MRS BEETON'S

Traditional

CHRISTMAS

RECIPES, GIFTS, CUSTOMS AND GAMES FROM A BYGONE ERA

Consultant Editor Bridget Jones

WARD LOCK

A WARD LOCK BOOK

First paperback edition published in 1994
by Ward Lock
Villiers House, 41/47 Strand, London WC2N 5JE

A Cassell Imprint

Edited by Jenni Fleetwood
Designed by Anita Ruddell
Photography by Sue Atkinson
Home Economists Gina Steer and Jacqui Hine
Craft Illustrations by Tony Randell

British Library Cataloguing-in-Publication Data
A catalogue record of this book is available from
the British Library

ISBN 0 7063 73073

Printed in Spain by Graficas Reunidas, S.a.. Madrid

CONTENTS

INTRODUCTION

This book brings together the Christmas recipes and traditions of Mrs Beeton's day with practical ideas and information for our contemporary celebrations. In spite of the trappings of modern society, everyone appreciates festive traditions which echo the true meaning of Christmas as a time for peace and friendship, warmth and celebration. The vast array of goods in the shops and instant entertainment in every home cannot replace the simple seasonal pleasures which have stood the test of time. From Mrs Beeton's day, and for generations before, they remain the focus for the celebration.

> *'Christmas Times of Queen Victoria, when amidst all our changes and progress, notwithstanding the rattling and whistling of the locomotive the noisy clatter of steam machinery on land and water; the marvels of the electric telegraph, photography, the printing press, and other wonders of this age; notwithstanding all these differences, Merrie Old Christmas still for his season reigns supreme.'*
>
> BEETON'S CHRISTMAS ANNUAL FOR 1860.

In Victorian homes, the onset of the Christmas season brought with it a flurry of preparation; from the kitchen to the parlour and nursery, every member of the household had a part to play. As always, the mistress of the house was the master of ceremonies, it was she who set about organising the whole event, from vital culinary aspects to the niceties of etiquette and entertaining. The kitchen was the centre of activity for some time before the approach of the day itself. Months before, the larder was stocked with preserves and the classic long-keeping dishes of the season. Lists were drawn up, orders placed, speciality foods secured and kitchen tasks carried out in readiness. All the equipment had to be in tip-top condition to cope with the cooking and feasting – the range was thoroughly cleaned, chimneys swept, pots scoured, serving dishes dusted and cutlery polished until it gleamed.

In the following chapters many of Mrs Beeton's original recipes are presented ready for use in today's kitchen – the quantities have been adjusted and the recipes re-tested to ensure not only that they work but also to confirm that the results are as impressive now as they were on the Victorian palate. There are menus and additional food ideas for each of the key days over the Christmas holiday; also celebration menus and food for simple gatherings are provided for the whole of the season, including entertaining during the weeks before Christmas.

As well as seeing that all was under way and in control below stairs, Mrs Beeton's contemporaries had a host of other commitments. Seated at their writing desks, the ladies had letters to write, good wishes to send, greetings to reciprocate, invitations to despatch, acceptances and apologies to make and special cards to send with loving messages. Some Christmas cards were made with care, embroidered in silk or delicately painted, and all greetings were beautifully written.

Many gifts, particularly special ones, were handmade. Throughout December men and boys would spend their time crafting items of woodwork while the ladies concentrated on embroidery, crochet

A festive table to greet guests, with warming Mulled Wine (page 30), Mince Pies (page 40) and Cheese Straws (page 22)

work and sewing. Even those gifts that were bought demanded special consideration in the choosing - specialist shops were visited and goods hand selected from neat counters and drawers of stock.

Although such minute attention to detail might not be the pattern today, it is as well to encourage all the family to take an active interest in Christmas preparations, at least by making decorations if not by devoting more time to making gifts. It is important to begin preparations a few weeks in advance, so that there is sufficient time to enjoy the activity without feeling frazzled by a last-minute rush. Why not substitute an evening of making cards, gift tags and decorations for one of inactivity in front of the television or allow the children to invite friends over one weekend to share in a simple gift-making session? Plan ahead so that you have all the materials needed – there's nothing more off-putting than running out of sticky paper strip or glue at a crucial moment. These Christmas preparations do not need to over-run the house and make it depressingly messy. Have a large cardboard box to hold all the materials at the end of every session and put all the finished items into another box for neat storage in a safe place.

Just as the Victorian housewife busied herself and family with the social round, do not forget the traditional entertaining and good cheer. Plan to have neighbours and acquaintances in for a Christmas drink, invite distant friends and relatives to visit and consider having a very special dinner party for those you will not otherwise see over the festive period. An early lunch party is an ideal way of entertaining both adults and children, or you might prefer to gather a chosen few together to help decorate the house and Christmas tree.

The tradition of extending goodwill to tradesmen has subsided but it is still jolly to greet regular callers with a small Christmas box of home-made biscuits or to offer hot mince pies or sausage rolls to those who visit the house. A century ago, out on the streets, chestnuts were roasted over fiery braziers and cheery greetings were shouted to passersby. You will still find the occasional barrow with hot chestnuts today; do not pass them by but perk up your spirits with this classic snack as you buy your presents.

'Christmas presents are being carried in all directions; numberless tons weight of turkeys, &c., load the railway carriages and other conveyances; merry are the groups of boys and girls from country schools; waggon-loads of holly, mistletoe, and other evergreens, fruits, and vegetables may be seen in the great markets; and in all parts are the Christmas viands, garnished with evergreens and ribbons, temptingly displayed; nor are the toy, grocers', and book shops without their attractions at this season.'

BEETON'S CHRISTMAS ANNUAL FOR 1860

Bringing in greenery is a long-standing tradition; a key event in Mrs Beeton's day. Holly, mistletoe, ivy, bay and other evergreens were brought into homes and churches were also decked with greenery. Even modest homes were hung with evergreens - great branches and wreaths, if not large trees. In fact, the Christmas tree was a recent arrival, 'a new phase in the observance of this national festival; for this pleasant aid to the sports of Christmas we are chiefly indebted to Prince Albert...' The Christmas tree was decorated with toys and sweets on Christmas Eve, and the family placed their presents around its base and on the branches.

There are alternatives to a Christmas tree. Beeton's Christmas Annual of 1862 included a detailed pattern and template for a sailing ship, to be built of wood and decoratively painted, then filled with gifts and displayed as a capital substitute for a tree. In the magazine the idea was introduced by a short story and there was also a song to be sung at the launch of the Christmas Ship. Although you may not have time to create such an elaborate decoration, and

may prefer to retain the traditional Christmas, festooning one room or a hallway with an alternative feature rings the changes.

On Christmas Day itself, Victorian adults and children alike would entertain the assembled company. Everyone planned and rehearsed some jovial contribution - songs, rhymes, stories, conjuring tricks or theatrical charades. Children and parents would together perform a short show and if the house was suitable there might be a makeshift stage and curtains too. Creating your own entertainment for Christmas Day is still an excellent idea, especially when there are a number of children in the party. After the first excitement of the day children are often overwhelmed by new toys, so having another focus for their attention is an excellent idea. Avoid the mistake of planning   long and complicated pieces. However, encouraging youngsters to sing a short song, play a short piece of music, recite a poem or act out a charade is fun, especially if adults join in and everyone keeps his or her own part a secret.

'In both town and country the church-bells ring on Christmas morning, and millions of voices join in prayer and praise in distant parts of the world, on sea and land: where no bells sound, the thoughts of them are a joyful memory, and many in the mind's eye fancy on this day the sound of ringing chimes, and of pleasant and well-remembered voices.'

BEETON'S CHRISTMAS ANNUAL FOR 1860

In spite of the hectic pace of modern life, try to think ahead for Christmas, allowing time to calm the bustle. Adopt a simpler approach to the many seasonal tasks. Make room for tradition, set aside time-out from technology and enjoy some of the simpler pleasures in the age-old spirit of Christmas.

CHRISTMAS BELLS

I.
O'er the air, so clear and frosty,
Swells a gladdening sound;
Christmas Bells, good tidings bringing,
Echo all around.
Calling every soul to hear
CHRISTMAS COMES BUT ONCE A YEAR

II.
Throb our hearts with deep emotion
As the Joy Bells ring;
Thronging mem'ries o'er our senses
Vision-like they fling.
Pealing through the midnight clear,
CHRISTMAS COMES BUT ONCE A YEAR

III.
Stars, the dark-blue Heaven bespangled,
Joy Bells in the air;
Their bright music helps the angels
Mortal joy to share.
PEACE ON EARTH – TO MEN GOOD-WILL
Christmas Bells are ringing still.

GILBERT PERCY.
BEETON'S CHRISTMAS ANNUAL 1861

COOK AHEAD FOR CHRISTMAS

Planning ahead for Christmas has never been easier – not only can the larder be stocked with traditional cook-ahead fare, such as the pudding, mincemeat, chutney and pickles, but a variety of other dishes can be prepared and frozen in readiness for the whole of the festive season. This section serves as a guide to the recipes which Mrs Beeton cooked ahead, and includes a selection of additional dishes which are practical candidates for forward planning.

Advance Planning

Making lists is the best way to plan for an important occasion. Begin by listing guests and meal occasions as well as the principal menus for the Christmas season. Next, make a list of useful dishes for freezing ahead, along with notes on when you anticipate serving them. If planning the festivities for the whole family generally falls to you, it saves time to keep the key lists from one year until the next - rather like a card list - so that they form the starting point for organising menus, games and so on. If you can bear the thought, it helps to jot down notes about particularly successful ideas on the lists before putting them away for the year.

Shopping Prepare shopping lists according to how far ahead you can buy the items as this spreads the cost as well as the work. For example, an early shopping list might include cards, presents and decorations as well as some foodstuffs, wine and other drinks. Make separate lists for bought frozen foods, canned and dried foods, and special items, such as luxury biscuits and confectionery. Remember to make a list of kitchen stationery or any unusual items which you might not normally buy. Lists of fresh foods and last-minute buys, can be added as you remember items. Not only is this easier than having one major planning session but it also reduces the likelihood of last-minute panics over forgotten purchases.

Household Preparations List all the tasks you hope to complete before Christmas. As well as any special cleaning or sorting out, think about linen which may need laundering in advance and any other domestic arrangements for guests who may be staying. If you have an open fire, have the chimney swept (ready for Father Christmas' descent) and stock up on fuel. Check items such as candles and paper napkins. Remember to buy spare bulbs for coloured tree lights and batteries for any gifts which may require them.

Food Preparation

Think in terms of three stages for advance food preparation: cooking several months ahead (either traditional preserves and storecupboard items or good freezer candidates), cooking 1-2 weeks in advance and cooking 1-2 days before Christmas.

Mincemeat, pickles and chutneys, rich fruit cake and plum pudding are all classic dishes to cook several months in advance. In addition, remember drinks such as home-made wines and liqueurs. Then, of course, there are the foods and dishes which freeze well and save time on last-minute preparation: bread, croissants, breadcrumbs, grated cheese, chopped fresh herbs, mashed potatoes (ideal for piping gratin borders), cooked chestnuts (puréed or whole), cooking apples and cranberries. Soups, casseroles, sauces, pasta dishes, pies, flans, cakes, teabreads and biscuits are useful freezer candidates for the Christmas period. Bought frozen items, such

Moulded Pudding (page 13) with Brandy Butter (page 29)

as seafood, vegetables, pastry, baked goods and cream may all be stocked up in advance. Selected foods may be prepared a week or two before they are required and stored quite successfully. Many crackers and biscuits keep well if they are stored in an airtight container in a cool place. Meringues keep well for several weeks in an airtight container. Flavoured butters, cranberry sauce, syrups and some salad dressings may be prepared and stored in airtight containers in the refrigerator. Some confectionery, such as chocolates, marzipan sweets and toffees, keeps well in a cool dry place.

Festive Arrangements

Finally, do enlist the assistance of family and friends who will be joining the household for Christmas with the preparations. Providing everyone with a role (no matter how small) in the preparation creates a team spirit and ensures that the whole household feels involved on Christmas day. Adopt a practical approach when delegating tasks - involve children in making decorations, enlist the support of an enthusiastic cook for making mince pies or ask one of the guests to make a bowl of punch for Christmas evening and so on. If you really neither want nor need practical help, ask for suggestions for family games.

CHRISTMAS PLUM-PUDDING IN MOULD.

PLAIN CHRISTMAS PUDDING

Originally, this plain pudding was intended for children. It is far lighter than the traditional rich pudding and is also unsweetened. It can be made up to a week ahead and stored in the refrigerator or prepared up to 6 months in advance and frozen.

fat for greasing (optional)
225 g/8 oz plain flour
225 g/8 oz fresh white breadcrumbs
175 g/6 oz raisins
175 g/6 oz currants
175 g/6 oz shredded suet
50 g/2 oz cut mixed peel
5 ml/1 tsp ground allspice
2 eggs
250 ml/8 fl oz milk
icing sugar for dredging

Prepare a floured pudding cloth or greased double-thick greaseproof paper and foil for wrapping the pudding. Three-quarters fill a large saucepan with water, set a steamer over the pan and bring the water to the boil.

Place the flour, breadcrumbs, raisins, currants, suet, peel and allspice in a mixing bowl. Beat the eggs with the milk, then pour this mixture into the dry ingredients and mix well until all the ingredients are thoroughly combined. Mound the mixture on the pudding cloth or on the greaseproof paper laid on a large sheet of foil. Press the mixture together into a round shape using the back of a metal spoon, then wrap it securely in the cloth or paper. Tie the cloth or fold the paper and foil to enclose the mixture completely.

Place the pudding in the steamer and cook over boiling water for 6 hours, topping up the pan with boiling water as required. Leave the pudding to cool, then wrap it in a fresh cloth or a double layer of clean greaseproof paper and foil or a polythene bag. Chill or freeze until required. Thaw a frozen pudding overnight. To reheat, steam the pudding for 2 hours. Dredge with icing sugar and top with holly.

SERVES SIX TO EIGHT

Moulded Pudding

ILLUSTRATED PAGE 11

Originally entitled 'An Unrivalled Plum-Pudding' and made in three-times the quantity given here, this pudding would have been boiled in a pudding cloth or in a tall, fluted mould. Cooking the pudding in a mould makes a attractive change from the usual basin - a deep fluted cake tin, kugel-hopf tin or dessert mould may be used. Do not store the pudding in a metal mould for a long period.

fat for greasing
225 g/8 oz raisins
250 g/9 oz currants
175 g/6 oz sultanas
275 g/10 oz soft dark brown sugar
275 g/10 oz fresh white breadcrumbs
275 g/10 oz shredded suet
50 g/2 oz cut mixed peel
grated rind of 1 lemon
15 ml/1 tbsp grated nutmeg
20 ml/4 tsp ground cinnamon
1.25 ml/¼ tsp almond essence
5 eggs
50 ml/2 fl oz brandy

Grease a 2.25 litre/4 pint boilable mould. Mix the raisins, currants, sultanas, sugar, breadcrumbs, suet, mixed peel, lemon rind, nutmeg and cinnamon. Beat the almond essence with the eggs and brandy, then stir the mixture into the dry ingredients and mix until thoroughly combined.

Turn the mixture into the prepared mould. Cover with greased greaseproof paper and foil. Stand the mould in a large saucepan and pour in boiling water to come halfway up the outside of the mould. Alternatively, the mould may be placed in a steamer set over a large saucepan of boiling water.

Boil the pudding for 6 hours, topping up the pan with boiling water as required. Leave the pudding to cool, then cover it with double-thick clean greaseproof paper and fresh foil. If a metal mould is used, the pudding should be turned out while still warm, cooled and wrapped in greaseproof paper and sealed in a polythene bag before storing.

Store the pudding in a cool, dry place until required. To reheat, replace in the greased mould if necessary and steam for a further 2 hours.

SERVES EIGHT TO TEN

Excellent Mincemeat

3 large cooking apples, cored
3 large lemons
450 g/1 lb raisins
450 g/1 lb currants
450 g/1 lb suet
900 g/2 lb soft light brown sugar
25 g/1 oz candied orange peel, chopped
25 g/1 oz candied citron or lemon peel, chopped
30 ml/2 tbsp orange marmalade
250 ml/8 fl oz brandy

Set the oven at 200°C/400°F/gas 6. Place the apples in an ovenproof dish, cover tightly and bake for 50-60 minutes, until thoroughly tender. Leave to cool.

Wash, dry and grate the lemons. Squeeze out the juice and reserve with the rind. Chop the shells, place them in a small saucepan and add cold water to cover. Bring to the boil, lower the heat and cover the pan. Simmer for about 1 hour, or until the shells are soft enough to chop very finely. Drain, cool and chop.

Scoop the apple flesh from the skins. Place it in a large bowl. Stir in the reserved lemon rind and juice with all the remaining ingredients. Cover the bowl and leave for 2 days, stirring occasionally. Pot, pressing the mincemeat down well. Cover tightly. Store for at least 2 weeks before using.

MAKES ABOUT 4 KG/9 LB

RICH CHRISTMAS PUDDING

The large quantity of sugar and dried fruit act as a preservative in Christmas pudding. Kept in a cool, dry, place, Christmas pudding will remain excellent for up to a year. Feed it occasionally with a little brandy.

fat for greasing
225 g/8 oz plain flour
pinch of salt
5 ml/1 tsp ground ginger
5 ml/1 tsp mixed spice
5 ml/1 tsp grated nutmeg
50 g/2 oz blanched almonds, chopped
400 g/14 oz soft dark brown sugar
225 g/8 oz shredded suet
225 g/8 oz sultanas
225 g/8 oz currants
200 g/7 oz seedless raisins
175 g/6 oz cut mixed peel
175 g/6 oz dried white breadcrumbs
6 eggs
75 ml/5 tbsp stout
juice of 1 orange
50 ml/2 fl oz brandy
125-250 ml/4-8 fl oz milk

Grease four 600 ml/1 pint pudding basins. Three-quarters fill four saucepans, each deep enough to hold a single pudding, with water.

Sift the flour, salt, ginger, mixed spice and nutmeg into a very large mixing bowl. Add the almonds, sugar, suet, dried fruit, peel and breadcrumbs.

In a second bowl, combine the eggs, stout, orange juice, brandy and 125 ml/4 fl oz milk. Mix well.

Stir the liquid mixture into the dry ingredients, adding more milk if necessary to give a soft dropping consistency. Divide the mixture between the pudding basins, covering each with greased greaseproof paper and foil. Secure with string.

Carefully lower the basins into the pans of boiling water. Cover the pans and lower the heat so that the water is kept at a steady simmer. Cook the puddings for 6-7 hours, topping up each pan with boiling water as required. The pudding basins should be covered at all times with boiling water.

After cooking, make sure that each pudding is dry and wrap it in clean greaseproof paper, then place it in an airtight container or seal it in a polythene bag. Foil may be used as an outer covering, over paper, but it should not come in direct contact with the pudding as the fruit acid causes it to break down and disintegrate to a coarse foil powder which ruins the surface of the pudding. To reheat, boil or steam each pudding for 1-2 hours. Serve with Brandy Butter (page 29) or Plum Pudding Sauce (page 92).

EACH PUDDING SERVES SIX

LEMON MINCEMEAT

2 large lemons
900 g/2 lb cooking apples, peeled, cored and minced
225 g/8 oz shredded suet
450 g/1 lb currants
225 g/8 oz sugar
75 g/3 oz candied citron and lemon or orange peel, chopped
10 ml/2 tsp mixed spice

Wash, dry and pare the lemons thinly, avoiding the pith. Place the rind in a small saucepan with water to cover. Bring to the boil, lower the heat and simmer for 15 minutes, or until the rind is tender. Drain and chop the rind. Squeeze the lemons and put the juice in a mixing bowl.

Add the apples to the bowl with the lemon rind, suet, currants, sugar, candied peel and spice. Stir well, cover tightly and leave for 1 week, stirring occasionally.

The mincemeat will be ready to use at the end of the week; however, it may be potted or put in containers, covered tightly and stored in a cool place for a further 2-3 weeks. It will also freeze well.

MAKES ABOUT 2.25 KG/5 LB

CHRISTMAS CAKE

This has been used for the Father Christmas Cake on page 19.

fat for greasing
200 g/7 oz plain flour
1.25 ml/¼ tsp salt
5-10 ml/1-2 tsp mixed spice
200 g/7 oz butter
200 g/7 oz caster sugar
6 eggs, beaten
30-60 ml/2-4 tbsp brandy or sherry
100 g/4 oz glacé cherries, chopped
50 g/2 oz preserved ginger, chopped
50 g/2 oz walnuts, chopped
200 g/7 oz currants · 200 g/7 oz sultanas
150 g/5 oz seedless raisins
75 g/3 oz cut mixed peel

COATING AND ICING
Almond Paste (page 17)
Royal Icing (page 17)

Line and grease a 20 cm/8 inch round or square cake tin. Use doubled greaseproof paper and tie a strip of brown paper around the outside. Set the oven at 160°C/325°F/gas 3.

Sift the flour, salt and spice into a bowl. In a mixing bowl, cream the butter and sugar together until light and fluffy. Gradually beat in the eggs and the brandy or sherry, adding a little flour if the mixture starts to curdle. Add the cherries, ginger and walnuts. Stir in the dried fruit, peel and flour mixture. Spoon into the prepared tin and make a slight hollow in the centre.

Bake for 45 minutes, then reduce the oven temperature to 150°C/300°F/gas 2 and bake for a further hour. Reduce the temperature still further to 140°C/275°F/gas 1, and continue cooking for 45-60 minutes until cooked through and firm to the touch. Cool in the tin. Cover with almond paste and decorate with royal icing.

MAKES ONE 20 CM/8 INCH CAKE

MRS BEETON'S CHRISTMAS CAKE

Taken from the first edition, this recipe is, in fact, a ginger-bread-type mixture which is enriched with cream and raisins. It may be made up to 3 months ahead and frozen or it will keep well in an airtight container for 2-3 weeks.

fat for greasing
575 g/1¼ lb plain flour
225 g/8 oz soft light brown sugar
30 ml/2 tbsp ground ginger
225 g/8 oz raisins, chopped
225 g/8 oz butter, melted
250 ml/8 fl oz single cream
250 ml/8 fl oz black treacle
2 eggs, lightly beaten
5 ml/1 tsp bicarbonate of soda
15 ml/1 tbsp vinegar
icing sugar for dredging

Line and grease a 25 cm/10 inch round cake tin. Set the oven at 160°C/325°F/gas 3. Mix the flour, sugar, ginger and raisins in a mixing bowl. Make a well in the dry ingredients, then add the butter, cream, treacle and eggs. Gradually beat the dry ingredients into the liquids, then continue beating until thoroughly combined.

Put the bicarbonate of soda in a cup, stir in the vinegar and immediately add this to the cake mixture. Beat well, then turn the mixture into the prepared tin. Bake for 2-2¼ hours, or until the cake is firm to the touch and cooked through.

Leave the cake to cool in the tin for 30 minutes, then transfer to a wire rack to cool completely. The cake is best stored in an airtight container for 1-2 days before eating. Dredge with icing sugar and top with a sprig of holly, if liked.

MAKES ONE 25 CM/10 INCH ROUND CAKE

BLACK BUN

400 g/14 oz plain flour
100 g/4 oz blanched whole almonds, roughly chopped
675 g/1½ lb muscatel raisins, seeded
675 g/1½ lb currants
100 g/4 oz cut mixed peel
200 g/7 oz caster sugar
30 ml/2 tbsp ground ginger
30 ml/2 tbsp ground cinnamon
30 ml/2 tbsp mixed spice
2.5 ml/½ tsp freshly ground black pepper
10 ml/2 tsp bicarbonate of soda
5 ml/1 tsp cream of tartar
250 ml/8 fl oz milk
15 ml/1 tbsp brandy

PASTRY
450 g/1 lb plain flour
225 g/ 8 oz butter
5 ml/1 tsp baking powder
flour for rolling out
beaten egg for glazing

Sift the flour into a large bowl. Add the almonds, dried fruit, peel, sugar and spices and mix well. Stir in the bicarbonate of soda and the cream of tartar, then moisten with the milk and brandy. Set the oven at 200°C/400°F/gas 6.

Make the pastry. Put the flour into a mixing bowl. Rub in the butter until the mixture resembles fine breadcrumbs, then add the baking powder. Stir in enough water (about 125 ml/4 fl oz) to form a stiff dough. Leave the dough to rest for a few minutes, then roll out on a lightly floured surface to a thickness of about 5 mm/¼ inch. Using three-quarters of the pastry, line a 23 cm/9 inch round cake tin (about 10 cm/4 inches deep), leaving a border for overlap. Roll out the remaining pastry for the lid.

Fill the pastry-lined tin with the cake mixture and turn the edges of the pastry over it. Moisten the edges with water, put on the lid and seal. Decorate the pastry with any trimmings, prick with a fork all over the top and brush with egg.

Bake for 1 hour, then lower the oven temperature to 160°C/325°F/gas 3, cover the top of the bun loosely with paper or foil. Bake for 2 hours more.

Leave the bun in the tin for 20 minutes, then remove it from the tin and cool completely. Keep for 1 month in an airtight tin before using.

MAKES ONE 23 CM/9 INCH CAKE

DUNDEE CAKE

ILLUSTRATED ON PAGE 27

fat for greasing
200 g/7 oz plain flour
2.5 ml/½ tsp baking powder
1.25 ml/¼ tsp salt
150 g/5 oz butter
150 g/5 oz caster sugar
4 eggs, beaten
100 g/4 oz glacé cherries, quartered
150 g/5 oz currants
150 g/5 oz sultanas
100 g/4 oz seedless raisins
50 g/2 oz cut mixed peel
50 g/2 oz ground almonds
grated rind of 1 lemon
50 g/2 oz blanched split almonds

Line and grease an 18 cm/7 inch round cake tin. Set the oven at 180°C/350°F/gas 4. Sift the flour, baking powder and salt into a bowl. In a mixing bowl, cream the butter and sugar together well, and beat in the eggs. Fold the flour mixture, cherries, dried fruit, peel and ground almonds into the creamed mixture. Add the lemon rind and mix well.

Spoon into the prepared tin and make a slight hollow in the centre. Bake for 20 minutes, by which time the hollow should have filled in. Arrange the split almonds on top.

Return the cake to the oven, bake for a further 40-50 minutes, then reduce the temperature to 160°C/325°F/gas 3 and bake for 1 hour more. Cool.

MAKES ONE 18 CM/7 INCH CAKE

Almond Paste

225 g/8oz ground almonds
100 g/4 oz caster sugar
100 g/4 oz icing sugar
5 ml/1 tsp lemon juice
few drops of almond essence
1 egg, beaten

Using a coarse sieve, sift the almonds, caster sugar and icing sugar into a mixing bowl. Add the lemon juice, almond essence and sufficient egg to bind the ingredients together. Knead lightly with the finger-tips until smooth. Wrap in cling film and overwrap in foil or a plastic bag to prevent the paste drying out. Store in a cool place.

MAKES ABOUT 450 G/1 LB

Royal Icing

It is vital to ensure that the bowl is clean and free from grease. Use a wooden spoon kept solely for the purpose and do not be tempted to skimp on the beating - insufficient beating will produce an off-white icing with a heavy texture.

2 egg whites
450g/1 lb icing sugar, sifted.

Place the egg whites in a bowl and break them up with a fork. Gradually beat in about two-thirds of the icing sugar with a wooden spoon, and continue beating for about 15 minutes until the icing is pure white and forms soft peaks. Add the remaining icing sugar, if necessary, to attain this texture. Cover the bowl with cling film and place a dampened tea-towel on top. Place the bowl inside a polythene bag if storing overnight or for longer.

Before use, lightly beat the icing to burst any air bubbles that have risen to the surface. Adjust the consistency for flat icing or piping.

SUFFICIENT TO COAT THE TOP AND SIDES
OF ONE 20CM/8 INCH CAKE.

ALMOND PASTE QUANTITIES

ROUND	QUANTITY
15 cm/6 inches	350 g/12 oz
18 cm/7 inches	500 g/18 oz
20 cm/8 inches	575 g/1¼ lb
23 cm/9 inches	800 g/1¾ lb
25 cm/10 inches	900 g/2 lb
28 cm/11 inches	1 kg/2¼ lb
30 cm/12 inches	1.25 kg/2¾ lb

SQUARE	QUANTITY
15 cm/6 inches	500 g/18 oz
18 cm/7 inches	575 g/1¼ lb
20 cm/8 inches	800 g/1¾ lb
23 cm/9 inches	900 g/2 lb
25 cm/10 inches	1 kg/2¼ lb
28 cm/11 inches	1.1 kg/2½ lb
30 cm/12 inches	1.4 kg/3 lb

ROYAL ICING QUANTITIES

(sufficient for 3 coats)

ROUND	QUANTITY
15 cm/6 inch	575 g/1¼ lb
18 cm/7 inch	675 g/1½ lb
20 cm/8 inch	800 g/1¾ lb
23 cm/9 inch	900 g/2 lb
25 cm/10 inch	1 kg/2¼ lb
28 cm/11 inch	1.25 kg/2¾ lb
30 cm/12 inch	1.4 kg/3 lb

SQUARE	QUANTITY
15 cm/6 inch	675 g/1½ lb
18 cm/7 inch	800 g/1¾ lb
20 cm/8 inch	900g/2 lb
23 cm/9 inch	1 kg/2¼ lb
25 cm/10 inch	1.25 kg/2¾ lb
28 cm/11 inch	1.4 kg/3 lb
30 cm/12 inch	1.5 kg/3¼ lb

COVERING THE CHRISTMAS CAKE WITH ALMOND PASTE

Lightly dust the work surface with icing sugar and brush the top of the cake with apricot glaze (see Mrs Beeton's Tip) or alcohol.

Lightly knead about one-third of the almond paste and roll it out evenly to 2.5 cm/1 inch larger than the top of the cake. Invert the cake, glazed side downwards, on to the paste.

Using a palette knife, carefully work round the edge of the cake, pushing and easing the paste under the cake to fill the gap. This ensures that the paste will be level. Trim off any excess paste where necessary then carefully turn the cake over, making sure that the almond paste is not left behind on the work surface. Centre the cake, paste-side uppermost, on a cake board.

To Cover the Sides

Measure the height of the cake accurately with a piece of string. Measure the circumference with string and add on 1 cm/½ inch to compensate for the thickness of the almond paste. From a sheet of parchment, cut a paper pattern that measures twice the height and half the circumference of the cake. Lightly dust the pattern with icing sugar. Brush the sides of the cake to remove all crumbs.

Lightly knead the remaining almond paste and shape it into a flat sausage the same length as the pattern. Place the paste down the middle of the paper pattern. Flatten the roll, then roll it out evenly across the width to fit the pattern exactly. Trim the edges, if necessary. With a sharp knife, cut the strip of paste in half along its length to make two equal strips, then following the cutting line, cut the paper in half with scissors.

Position the cake in the middle of the cake board and brush apricot glaze or alcohol around the side. Lift up one strip of paste on the paper and place it in position around the cake. Repeat with the second piece. Carefully remove the paper and smooth the joins. Smooth around the cake with your hands to press the almond paste securely on to the cake.

Square Cakes Attach the almond paste to a square cake as for a large round cake. It is easier if you avoid having the joins on the corners. Mould the corners neatly once the paste is in position and when the joins have been smoothed.

MRS BEETON'S TIP
To make Apricot Glaze, warm 225g/8oz apricot jam with 30ml/2 tbsp water in a small saucepan until the jam has melted. Sieve the mixture and return to the clean pan. Bring slowly to the boil. Cool.

APPLYING ROYAL ICING

Begin by coating the top of the cake with icing. Beat the icing well. Cover the top of the cake with icing, using a palette knife to work the icing evenly over the almond paste. Use a paddle-action to knock air bubbles out of the icing and make an even layer with regular ridge marks. Use an icing ruler or flat edge to smooth the top. Hold it with both hands at an acute angle to the surface and pull it across the icing in one smooth stroke. Use a knife to scrape off excess icing which overhangs the side of the cake. Leave to dry for 24 hours, then apply another two coats until the surface is smooth.

To flat ice the side, paddle on the icing as for the top, then use a side scraper to achieve a smooth finish. For a round cake, use a turntable: hold the side scraper still against the side of the cake and move the turntable through a complete rotation. On a square cake, flat ice two opposite sides, scraping the icing smooth and neatening the corners, then leave them to dry before icing the remaining sides.

Rough icing is a simple, effective covering for Christmas cakes. Cover the cake completely and evenly with icing, then pull it into peaks with the end of the blade of a palette knife.

Alternatively, for a smooth finish, buy sugarpaste or roll-out icing. This is rolled out and draped over the almond paste on the cake, then carefully moulded into the shape of the cake with the hands.

Father Christmas Cake

ILLUSTRATED ON PAGE 127

Prepare and paint the run-out for this cake in advance, allowing it to dry before placing it on the cake. Leftover royal icing is used to pipe the beard and fur trimmings.

20 cm/8 inch square Christmas Cake
(page 15), covered in Almond Paste
(page 17) and Royal Icing (page 17)
450 g/1 lb Royal Icing (page 17) for run-outs and piping
selection of food colourings
1.25 metres/4 feet red ribbon, about 4 cm/1½ inches wide

Using the template provided, either same size or enlarged, make a run-out Father Christmas. Use full strength royal icing for the outlines, thinning it with a little lemon juice or water for flooding. Numbers on the template indicate the order in which sections should be piped and flooded; allow each section to dry before piping the next. When the finished run-out is dry, paint it as shown in the photograph.

Place some of the remaining royal icing in an icing bag fitted with writing nozzle and pipe the greetings message (as shown in the photograph) on the cake. Top the Father Christmas run-out with Cornelli icing (scribbles) on the beard and trimmings. Leave to dry. Fit a shell nozzle on to a second bag of royal icing and pipe a border of shells or stars around the top and lower edge of the cake. Allow the icing to dry for several hours.

Using a dab of royal icing, stick the run-out in position. Place the ribbon around the Father Christmas cake, securing it at the back.

Colour a little of the remaining royal icing red. Place it in an icing bag fitted with the clean writing nozzle and pipe directly over the white writing to highlight the greetings.

ABOUT 30-35 PORTIONS

Trace this template, then it may be increased in size on a photocopier. Secure on a board and cover with wax paper. Flood the sections with royal icing.

FESTIVE LOG

fat for greasing
3 eggs
75 g/3 oz caster sugar
65 g/2½ oz plain flour
30 ml/2 tbsp cocoa
2.5 ml/½ tsp baking powder
pinch of salt
small piece of marzipan or moulding icing
red food colouring
chocolate leaves (see Mrs Beeton's Tip)

CHOCOLATE BUTTERCREAM
50 g/2 oz plain chocolate, grated
15 ml/1 tbsp milk
100 g/4 oz butter, softened
225 g/8 oz icing sugar, sifted

FROSTING
225 g/8 oz granulated sugar
pinch of cream of tartar
1 egg white
2.5 ml/½ tsp vanilla essence

Line and grease a 30 x 20 cm/12 x 8 inch Swiss roll tin. Set the oven at 220°C/425°F/gas 7. Combine the eggs and sugar in a heatproof bowl. Place over a saucepan of simmering water. Whisk for 10-15 minutes until thick and creamy, then remove from the heat and continue whisking until the mixture is cold.

Sift the flour, cocoa, baking powder and salt into a bowl, then lightly fold into the egg mixture. Pour into the prepared tin and bake for 10 minutes.

When the cake is cooked, turn it on to a large sheet of greaseproof paper dusted with caster sugar. Peel off the lining paper. Trim any crisp edges. Place a second piece of greaseproof paper on top of the cake and roll up tightly from one long side, with the paper inside. Cool completely on a wire rack.

Meanwhile make the buttercream. Combine the chocolate and milk in a heatproof bowl. Stir over hot water until dissolved, then set aside to cool. Cream the butter in a mixing bowl, gradually add the chocolate mixture and work in the icing sugar. Beat the buttercream until light and fluffy. Unroll the cold cake, remove the paper, spread with the buttercream and roll up again. Place on a cake board.

Make the frosting by combining the sugar, cream of tartar and 60 ml/4 tbsp water in a small saucepan. Heat gently, stirring until the sugar has dissolved, then raise the heat and cook without stirring until the syrup registers 115°C/240°F on a sugar thermometer, or when 2.5 ml/½ tsp of the syrup dropped into a bowl of iced water forms a soft ball which can be moulded. Remove from the heat.

Whisk the egg white in a large grease-free bowl until stiff. Pour on the syrup in a thin stream, whisking constantly. Add the vanilla essence and continue to whisk until the frosting is thick and glossy and stands in peaks when the whisk is lifted.

Quickly spread the frosting over the chocolate roll, making sure it comes well down on each side. As the frosting begins to set, draw a fork or serrated scraper down the length of the cake. Swirl the icing on the ends of the roll into circles. Colour the marzipan red, roll it into berries and use with the chocolate leaves to decorate the log.

ABOUT 10 PORTIONS

MRS BEETON'S TIP
To make chocolate leaves, select clean dry non-poisonous leaves such as rose leaves. Brush the underside of each leaf with melted chocolate. Dry the leaves, chocolate-side uppermost, then carefully peel away the leaves.

Christmas Stollen

This is the classic German Christmas bread. It will remain fresh for many weeks if well wrapped in foil or greaseproof paper and stored in an airtight tin.

butter for greasing
1 kg/2¼ lb plain flour
75 g/3 oz yeast
200 ml/7 fl oz lukewarm milk
350 g/12 oz butter
grated rind and juice of 1 lemon
250 g/9 oz caster sugar
2 egg yolks
5 ml/1 tsp salt
500 g/18 oz seedless raisins
225 g/8 oz sultanas
150 g/5 oz blanched slivered almonds
100 g/4 oz chopped mixed peel
flour for dusting
100 g/4 oz unsalted butter
icing sugar for dusting

Butter a baking sheet. Sift the flour into a bowl. Blend the yeast with the warm milk and 50 g/2 oz of the flour. Set aside until frothy.

Meanwhile, melt the butter. Cool slightly, then blend into the remaining flour with the lemon juice. Add the milk and yeast liquid together with the lemon rind, sugar, egg yolks and salt. Beat well together. Knead the dough until it is very firm and elastic, and leaves the sides of the bowl. Cover with cling film. Leave in a warm place until the dough has doubled in bulk. This will take about 2 hours.

Meanwhile, mix the dried fruit with the nuts and mixed peel. Knead the dough again, pull the sides to the centre, turn it over and cover once more. Leave to rise for a further 30 minutes. When the dough has doubled in bulk again, turn it on to a floured surface and knead in the fruit and nut mixture.

Divide the dough in half and roll each half into a pointed oval shape. Lay each on the prepared baking sheet. Place a rolling pin along the length of each piece of the dough in the centre. Roll half the dough lightly from the centre outwards. Brush the thinner rolled half with a little water and fold the other half over it, leaving a margin of about 5 cm/2 inches all around which allows for the dough to rise. Press well together; the water will bind it. Cover the stollen and leave to rise in a warm place until doubled in bulk again. Set the oven at 190°C/375°F/gas 5.

Melt 50 g/2 oz of the unsalted butter and brush it over the stollen. Bake for about 1 hour, until golden. When baked, melt the remaining unsalted butter, brush it over the stollen, then sprinkle with icing sugar. Keep for at least a day before cutting.

MAKES TWO LOAVES, ABOUT 24 SLICES EACH

Oatcakes

fat for greasing
50 g/2 oz bacon fat or dripping
100 g/4 oz medium oatmeal
1.25 ml/¼ tsp salt
1.25 ml/¼ tsp bicarbonate of soda
fine oatmeal for rolling out

Grease two baking sheets. Set the oven at 160°C/325°F/gas 3.

Melt the bacon fat or dripping in a large saucepan. Remove from the heat and stir in the dry ingredients, then add enough boiling water to make a stiff dough.

When cool enough to handle, knead the dough thoroughly, then roll out on a surface dusted with fine oatmeal, to a thickness of 5 mm/¼ inch. Cut into wedge-shaped pieces and transfer to the prepared baking sheets. Bake for 20-30 minutes. Cool on a wire rack. Store in an airtight container.

MAKES ABOUT 16

CHEESE STRAWS

ILLUSTRATED ON PAGE 7

fat for greasing
100 g/4 oz plain flour
pinch of mustard powder
pinch of salt
pinch of cayenne pepper
75 g/3 oz butter
75 g/3 oz grated Parmesan cheese
1 egg yolk
flour for rolling out

Grease four baking sheets. Set the oven at 200°C/400°F/gas 6.

Sift the flour, mustard, salt and cayenne into a bowl. In a mixing bowl, cream the butter until soft and white, then add the flour mixture with the cheese. Stir in the egg yolk and enough cold water to form a stiff dough.

Roll out on a lightly floured surface to a thickness of about 5 mm/¼ inch and cut into fingers, each measuring about 10 x 1 cm/4 inches x ½ inch. From the pastry trimmings make several rings, each about 4 cm/1½ inches in diameter.

With a palette knife, transfer both rings and straws to the prepared baking sheets and bake for 8-10 minutes or until lightly browned and crisp. Cool on the baking sheets.

When serving, fit a few straws through each ring and lay the bundles in the centre of a plate with any remaining straws criss-crossed around them.

MAKES 48 TO 60

PICCALILLI

ILLUSTRATED OPPOSITE

This colourful pickle is made from a variety of vegetables. In addition to the selection below, chopped peppers (green, yellow and red), young broad beans, shallots or marrow may be used. The prepared mixed vegetables should weigh about 1 kg/2 ¼ lb.

450 g/1 lb green tomatoes, diced
½ small firm cauliflower, broken into florets
1 small cucumber, peeled, seeded and cubed
2 onions, roughly chopped
100 g/4 oz firm white cabbage, shredded
50 g/2 oz cooking salt
750 ml/1¼ pints vinegar
12 chillies
225 g/8 oz sugar
25 g/1 oz mustard powder
15 g/½ oz turmeric
30 ml/2 tbsp cornflour

Combine all the vegetables in a large bowl, sprinkle with the salt, cover and leave to stand for 24 hours. Rinse thoroughly, then drain well.

Heat the vinegar in a saucepan with the chillies. Boil for 2 minutes, leave to stand for 30 minutes, then strain the vinegar into a jug and allow to cool.

Combine the sugar, mustard, turmeric and cornflour in a large bowl. Mix to a paste with a little of the cooled vinegar. Bring the rest of the vinegar back to the boil in a saucepan, pour over the blended mixture, return to the pan; boil for 3 minutes.

Remove from the heat, stir in the drained vegetables, pack into clean jars and seal at once with vinegar-proof covers.

MAKES ABOUT 1 KG/2 ¼ LB

Preserves to cook ahead for Christmas: Clementines in Vodka (page 28), Piccalilli (page 22), Apple Chutney (page 24) and Quick Candied Peel (page 29)

PICKLED HORSERADISH

horseradish roots
vinegar
salt

Wash the roots in hot water, peel off the skin, then either grate or mince them. Pack loosely in small clean jars.

Horseradish does not need to be soaked in brine, but 5 ml/1 tsp salt should be added to each 250 ml/8 fl oz vinegar used for filling the jars. Pour the salted vinegar over the horseradish to cover, close the jars with vinegar-proof lids and store in a cool, dark place.

MRS BEETON'S TIP
A variety of covers are vinegar-proof and thus suitable for pickles and chutneys. The most obvious choice are the twist-top or screw-on plastic-coated lids used commercially. Press-on plastic covers are also suitable. Alternatively, cut a circle of clean card or paper to the size of the top of the jar. Set it in place and cover with a piece of linen dipped in melted paraffin wax. Tie the linen firmly in place.

PICKLED WALNUTS

One of the most delicious pickles and an integral part of the Boxing Day cold table. Use green walnuts whose shells have not begun to form. Wear gloves when handling the walnuts to avoid staining your hands. Prick well with a stainless steel fork; if the shell can be felt – and it begins forming opposite the stalk, about 5 mm/ inch from the end – do not use.

soft green walnuts
brine in the proportion 100 g/4 oz salt to 1 litre/1¾ pints water
Spiced Vinegar (see Mrs Beeton's Tip)

Place the pricked walnuts in a large bowl, cover with brine and leave to soak for about 6 days. Drain, cover

with a fresh solution of brine and leave to soak for 7 days more. Drain again and spread in a single layer on greaseproof paper. Cover loosely with more paper, then leave, preferably in sunshine for 1–2 days or until blackened.

Pack into warm clean jars. Bring the spiced vinegar to the boil and fill the jars. When cold, put on vinegar-proof covers. Store in a cool dark place for at least 1 month before using.

MRS BEETON'S TIP
To make Spiced Vinegar, crush 7 g/¼ oz each of cloves, allspice berries, broken cinnamon sticks and bruised root ginger in a clean cloth. Tip the spices into a jug and add 1 litre/1 ¾ pints white or malt vinegar. Mix well, pour into a 1.1 litre/2 pint bottle, seal tightly and shake daily for 1 month. Store in a cool dry place for at least 1 month more before straining out the spices. Return the vinegar to the clean bottle. Use as required in pickles, dressings and sauces.

APPLE CHUTNEY

ILLUSTRATED ON PAGE 23

3 kg/6½ lb apples
2 litres/3½ pints vinegar
1.5 kg/3¼ lb sugar · 25 g/1 oz salt
10 ml/2 tsp ground allspice
300-400 g/11-14oz preserved ginger, chopped
1 kg/2¼ lb sultanas, chopped

Peel and core the apples; chop them into small pieces. Combine the vinegar, sugar, salt and allspice in a saucepan or preserving pan. Bring to the boil, add the apples, lower the heat and simmer for 10 minutes.

Add the ginger and sultanas to the pan and simmer the mixture until fairly thick. Pour into warm clean jars and cover with vinegar-proof lids. When cool, wipe the jars, label and store in a cool dry place.

MAKES ABOUT 5 KG/11 LB

SPICED PEACH PICKLE

This is particularly good with cold baked ham.

2 kg/4½ lb peaches, peeled
20 g/¾ oz whole cloves
20 g/¾ oz allspice berries
1 cinnamon stick, broken in short lengths
1 kg/2¼ lb sugar
1 litre/1¾ pints distilled vinegar

Cut the peaches in half. Remove the stones, crack a few of them and put the kernels in a small saucepan. Add water to cover, bring to the boil and blanch for 3 minutes. Drain.

Tie the spices in muslin and place with the sugar and vinegar in a preserving pan or heavy-bottomed saucepan. Heat gently to dissolve the sugar, then bring to the boil. Lower the heat, stir in the peaches, and simmer until the fruit is just tender, but not overcooked or broken.

Using a slotted spoon, transfer the peach halves to warm clean jars, adding a few of the blanched kernels to each. Continue to boil the liquid in the pan until it thickens, then remove the bag of spices and pour the liquid into the jars. Put on vinegar-proof covers while hot. When cold, label and store in a cool dark place for at least a week.

MAKES ABOUT 3.25 KG/7 LB

CHEROKEE SAUCE

A potent sauce for pepping up gravies and savoury mixtures, such as hashed turkey, turkey croquettes or ham loaf.

15 ml/1 tbsp cayenne pepper
5 garlic cloves, crushed
30 ml/2 tbsp soy sauce
15 ml/1 tbsp walnut ketchup or 1 pickled walnut, crushed
600 ml/1 pint malt vinegar

Combine all the ingredients in a saucepan. Bring to the boil, lower the heat and simmer very gently for 30 minutes.

Heat sufficient clean bottles to hold the sauce; prepare vinegar-proof lids. Fill the hot bottles with the sauce and cover. Label when cold.

MAKES ABOUT 450 ML/¾ PINT

'CINNAMON - The cinnamon-tree (Laurus Cinnamomum) is a valuable and beautiful species of the laurel family, and grows to the height of 20 or 30 feet. The trunk is short and straight, with wide-spreading branches, and it has a smooth ash-like bark. The leaves are upon short stalks and are of an oval shape, and 3 to 5 inches long. The flowers are in panicles, with six small petals, and the fruit is about the size of an olive, soft, insipid, and of a deep blue. This incloses a nut, the kernel of which germinates soon after it falls. The wood of the tree is white and not very solid, and its root is thick and branching, exuding a great quantity of camphor. The inner bark of the tree forms the cinnamon of commerce. Ceylon was thought to be its native island but it has been found in Malabar, Cochin-china, Sumatra, and the Eastern Islands; also in the Brazils, the Mauritius, Jamaica, and other Tropical localities.'

MRS BEETON (1861)

CHRISTOPHER NORTH'S SAUCE

Serve this potent sauce as a relish with roast beef, veal or game, or use it to pep up gravies and other sauces.

175 ml/6 fl oz port
30 ml/2 tbsp Worcestershire sauce
10 ml/2 tsp mushroom ketchup
10 ml/2 tsp caster sugar
15 ml/1 tbsp lemon juice
1.25 ml/¼ tsp cayenne pepper
2.5 ml/½ tsp salt

Mix all the ingredients together in the top of a double saucepan or a heatproof bowl set over simmering water. Heat gently, without boiling. Serve at once or cool quickly and refrigerate in a closed jar.

MAKES ABOUT 250 ML/8 FL OZ

AN EXCELLENT PICKLE

This recipe was forwarded to Mrs Beeton by a subscriber of The Englishwoman's Domestic Magazine. It is an unusual pickle by comparison with recipes which are today popular; however, its crunchy texture and piquant flavour complement cold roast beef or pork, boiled or baked ham, or full-flavoured cheese. The pickle may be eaten on the day it is made or may be kept for up to a month.

1 onion, thinly sliced
½ cucumber, peeled and thinly sliced
1 cooking apple, peeled, quartered,
cored and sliced
7.5 ml/1½ tsp salt
cayenne pepper
125 ml/4 fl oz cream sherry
125 ml/4 fl oz soy sauce
about 150 ml/¼ pint cider vinegar

Layer the onion, cucumber and apple in a large perfectly clean jar. Sprinkle each layer with salt and cayenne pepper. Originally, 3.75 ml/¾ tsp cayenne was suggested - this makes the pickle extremely hot so reduce this to taste. A pinch of cayenne is sufficient to pep up the whole jar of pickle.

Pour the sherry and soy sauce over the vegetables, then add sufficient cider vinegar to cover them completely. Cover with a vinegar-proof airtight lid and invert the jar once or twice to make sure the soaking liquid is well mixed. Leave to stand for at least 1 hour before use. Store in a cool, dark place.

MAKES ONE 1 KG/2¼ LB JAR

The following quote from the first edition of Mrs Beeton's Book of Household Management highlights the author's cosmopolitan approach to food. Her comment on the fact that Chinese and Japanese soy sauces are different is still valid. The Chinese sauce is not suitable for use in Japanese dishes as the latter sauce has a finer flavour.

'Soy - This is a sauce frequently made use of for fish, and comes from Japan, where it is prepared from the seeds of a plant called Dolichos Soja. The Chinese also manufacture it; but that made by the Japanese is said to be the best. All sorts of statements have been made respecting the very general adulteration of this article in England, and we fear that many of them are too true. When genuine, it is of an agreeable flavour, thick, and of a clear brown colour.'

MRS BEETON (1861)

*Less rich than an iced cake,
Dundee Cake (page 16) is a
traditional Christmas treat*

Apricots in Brandy

1.8 kg/4 lb apricots
225 g/8 oz sugar
250 ml/8 fl oz brandy

You will need three (450 g/1 lb) preserving jars. Sterilize the jars (see Mrs Beeton's Tip right) and drain thoroughly, then warm in an oven set at 120°C/250°F/gas ½. Wash and drain the apricots and prick them with a sterilized darning needle. Pour 300 ml/½ pint water into a large heavy-bottomed saucepan or preserving pan. Add 100 g/4 oz of the sugar; heat gently, stirring, until dissolved.

Add enough of the apricots to cover the base of the pan in a single layer. Bring the syrup back to the boil and remove the riper fruit at once. Firmer fruit should be boiled for 2 minutes, but do not let it become too soft. As the fruit is ready, transfer it to the warmed jars, using a slotted spoon.

Set the oven at 150°C/300°F/gas 2. Add the remaining sugar to the syrup in the pan, lower the temperature and stir until the sugar has dissolved. Boil the syrup, without stirring, until it registers 105°C/220°F on a sugar thermometer, the thread stage. Alternatively, test by dipping a teaspoon in the syrup and then pressing another spoon on to the back of it and pulling away. If a thread forms, the syrup is ready. Remove the syrup from the heat.

Measure out 250 ml/8 fl oz of the syrup. Stir in the brandy, then pour the mixture over the apricots, covering them completely, and filling the jars to within 2 cm/½ inch of the top.

Dip rubber rings (if used) and lids in boiling water and fit them on the jars. Do not fit clips or screw bands. Line a roasting tin with three or four layers of newspaper. Stand the jars 5 cm/2 inches apart on the newspaper. Put the jars in the middle of the oven and process for 40-50 minutes.

Prepare a clean, dry wooden surface on which to stand the jars. Immediately check that the necks of the jars are clean, wiping them with absorbent kitchen paper, and fit the screw bands or clips. **Do not wipe the jars with a damp cloth or they will crack.**

Leave for 24 hours before testing the seal by removing the screw bands or clips and lifting the jars by their lids. If the lids stay firm they are properly sealed. Label and store for at least 1 month.

MAKES ABOUT 1.4 KG/3 LB

Clementines in Vodka

ILLUSTRATED ON PAGE 23

1 kg/2¼ lb clementines
100 g/4 oz caster sugar
600 ml/1 pint water · ½ vanilla pod
30 ml/2 tbsp orange flower water
300 ml/½ pint vodka

Remove the leaves, stalks and flower-ends from the clementines. Prick them all over with a sterilized darning needle - this helps the syrup to penetrate the skins.

Combine the sugar, water and vanilla pod in a saucepan. Place over low heat, stirring occasionally until the sugar has dissolved. Add the clementines, raise the heat and bring to the boil. Lower the heat and simmer, uncovered, for about 25 minutes, until the fruit is tender. Remove the vanilla pod.

Drain the fruit, reserving the syrup. Pack the fruit into two warm, sterilized jars (see Mrs Beeton's Tip). Divide the vodka between them, then fill up the jars with the syrup. Seal the jars and tilt them gently to blend the liquids. Store in a cool, dry place for at least four weeks before opening.

MAKES ABOUT 1 KG/2¼ LB

MRS BEETON'S TIP

To sterilize jars, wash in hot soapy water, rinse well, then stand them on slats of wood, a rack or a pad of paper in a deep saucepan. Pour in cold water to cover the jars completely. Put the jar lids into the pan. Heat gently until the water boils, then boil the jars for 5 minutes. Turn off the heat. Leave the jars submerged until they are required, then drain upside down on clean tea towels. Althernatively, use one of the sterilizing products developed for wine making.

Quick Candied Peel

ILLUSTRATED ON PAGE 23

Soak grapefruit or lemon peel overnight to extract some of the bitterness. Cut the peel into long strips, 5 mm/¼ inch wide. Put in a saucepan, cover with cold water and bring slowly to the boil. Drain, add fresh water and bring to the boil again. Drain, and repeat 3 more times. Weigh the cooled peel and place with an equal quantity of sugar in a pan. Just cover with boiling water, and boil gently until the peel is tender and clear. Cool, strain from the syrup, and toss the peel in caster or granulated sugar on greaseproof paper. Spread out on a wire rack to dry for several hours. Roll again in sugar if at all sticky. When quite dry, store in covered jars. Use within 3-4 months.

Cumberland Rum Butter

100 g/4 oz unsalted butter
100 g/4 oz soft light brown sugar
30 ml/2 tbsp rum
2.5 ml/½ tsp grated orange rind
grated nutmeg

Put the butter in a bowl and cream it until very soft and light-coloured. Crush any lumps in the sugar. Work it into the butter until completely blended in.

Work the rum into the butter, a few drops at a time, take care not to let the mixture separate. Mix in the orange rind. Taste the mixture and add a little grated nutmeg.

Pile the rum butter into a dish, and leave to firm up before serving; or turn lightly into a screw-topped jar and store in a cool place until required. Use within 4 days, or refrigerate for longer storage. Bring to room temperature before serving.

MAKES ABOUT 225 G/8 OZ

Orange Liqueur Butter

grated rind of 2 oranges
4 sugar lumps
150 g/5 oz butter, softened
25 g/1 oz caster sugar
15 ml/1 tbsp orange juice, strained
20 ml/4 tsp Cointreau

Put the orange rind in a bowl and mix it with the sugar lumps. Work in the butter and caster sugar until well blended.

Stir in the juice and liqueur gradually, until fully absorbed. Use at once, or pot, cover tightly and chill.

MAKES ABOUT 175 G/6 OZ

Brandy Butter

ILLUSTRATED ON PAGE 11

50 g/2 oz butter
100 g/4 oz caster sugar
15-30 ml/1-2 tbsp brandy

In a bowl, cream the butter until soft. Gradually beat in the sugar until the mixture is pale and light. Work in the brandy, a little at a time, taking care not to allow the mixture to curdle. Chill before using. If the mixture has separated slightly after standing, beat well before serving.

MAKES ABOUT 150 G\5 OZ

VARIATIONS

Sherry Butter Make as for Brandy Butter but substitute sherry for the brandy. Add a stiffly beaten egg white, if a softer texture is preferred.
Vanilla Butter Make as for Brandy Butter but substitute 5 ml/1 tsp vanilla essence for the brandy.
Orange or Lemon Butter Cream the grated rind of 1 orange or lemon with the butter and sugar, then gradually beat in 15 ml/1 tbsp orange juice or 5 ml/1 tsp lemon juice. Omit the brandy.

FESTIVE DRINKS

ℛUM AND BRANDY TODDY

225 g/8 oz sugar lumps
2 large lemons
600 ml/1 pint rum
600 ml/1 pint brandy
5 ml/1 tsp grated nutmeg

Rub a few of the sugar lumps over the lemons to absorb the oil. Put them in a heatproof bowl with the remaining sugar lumps. Squeeze the lemons and strain the juice into the bowl, then crush the sugar with a wooden spoon.

Pour 1.1 litres/2 pints boiling water into the bowl, stir well, then add the remaining ingredients. Mix thoroughly. Serve at once.

SERVES EIGHT TO TEN

ℳULLED WINE

ILLUSTRATED ON PAGE 7

This traditional Christmas drink used to be heated by means of a red-hot mulling poker. Today the mixture is more likely to be made on top of the stove.

100 g/4 oz caster sugar
4 cinnamon sticks
4 cloves
1 nutmeg
2 oranges, thinly sliced
1 bottle red wine

Boil 600 ml/1 pint water with the sugar and spices in a saucepan for 5 minutes. Add the oranges, remove the pan from the heat and set aside for 15 minutes. Stir in the wine. Heat slowly without boiling. Serve very hot, in heated glasses.

SERVES EIGHT TO TEN

𝒩EGUS

Mrs Beeton used more water in the making of her Negus which was originally a drink served at children's parties. Sherry or sweet white wine were sometimes used instead of port.

100 g/4 oz sugar lumps
1 lemon
600 ml/1 pint port
grated nutmeg

Rub a few of the sugar lumps over the lemon to absorb the oil. Put all the sugar lumps in a large heatproof jug.

Squeeze the lemon and strain the juice into the jug. Pour in the port. Stir the mixture, crushing the sugar lumps. Add 600 ml/1 pint boiling water, with grated nutmeg to taste. Stir well to dissolve all the sugar, cover the jug and set aside to cool slightly before serving.

SERVES SIX TO EIGHT

SPIRITUOUS

'PUNCH:– Punch is a beverage made of various spirituous liquors or wine, hot water, the acid juice of fruits, and sugar. It is considered to be very intoxicating; but this is probably because the spirit, being partly sheathed by the mucilaginous juice and the sugars, its strength does not appear to the taste so great as it really is.'

MRS. BEETON (1861)

Mince Pies (page 40) and a pot of Brandy Butter (page 29)

Mulled Ale

1 litre/1¾ pints ale
15-30 ml/1-2 tbsp caster sugar
generous pinch of ground cloves
pinch of grated nutmeg
generous pinch of ground ginger
100 ml/3½ fl oz rum or brandy

Combine the ale, 15 ml/1 tbsp caster sugar and the spices in a large saucepan. Bring to just below boiling point. Remove from the heat and stir in the rum or brandy, with more sugar if required. Ladle into heated glasses and serve at once.

SERVES EIGHT TO TEN

Champagne Cup

12 ice cubes or the equivalent quantity of crushed ice
1.1 litres/2 pints champagne
75 ml/3 fl oz curacao
25 g/1 oz icing sugar
600 ml/1 pint soda water
10 cm/4 inch strip of cucumber peel

Put the ice in a large jug. Stir in the champagne, curacao and icing sugar. Add the soda water and decorate with the cucumber peel. Serve at once.

SERVES EIGHT TO TEN

Whiskey Cordial

450 g/1 lb ripe white currants
grated rind of 2 lemons
100 g/4 oz root ginger, grated
1.1 litres/2 pints whiskey
450 g/1 lb sugar lumps, crushed

Strip the currants from the stalks and put them in a large jug. Add the lemon rind, ginger and whiskey.

Cover the jug closely and set it aside for 24 hours.

Strain through a fine sieve into a clean jug, stir in the sugar lumps and leave to stand for 12 hours more, stirring occasionally to dissolve the sugar lumps. Pour into clean bottles, cork tightly and store in a cool dry place.

MAKES ABOUT 1.25 LITRES/2¼ PINTS

Claret Cup

8 ice cubes or the equivalent quantity of crushed ice
75 ml/3 fl oz maraschino liqueur
50 g/2 oz icing sugar
500 ml/17 fl oz soda water
1 orange, sliced
2-3 borage sprigs

Put the ice in a large jug. Stir in claret, maraschino and icing sugar. Just before serving, add the soda water and decorate with orange slices and borage.

SERVES FOUR TO SIX

Strawberries in Sherry

Strawberries macerated in sherry make a delicious addition to punches and wine cups. Although the friut softens and darkens in colour, with its rich strawberry-flavoured syrup, it is ideal as a last-minute dessert sauce, while the filled jars make attractive presents.

900 g/2 lb strawberries
100 g/4 oz caster sugar
dry sherry (see method)

The fruit should be in perfect condition; clean, dry and hulled. Place the strawberries in sterilized wide-necked jars, sprinkling the sugar over the layers. The jars should be filled, but not overflowing.

Pour sherry into the jars to fill them completely, covering the fruit. Tap the jars on the work sur-

face to release any air bubbles. Cover tightly and set aside for 2-3 days, then top up with more liquor if necessary. Leave for at least 2 weeks before using.

MAKES ABOUT 900 G/2 LB

HOME MADE NOYEAU

This nut-flavoured liqueur can be used to flavour puddings and cakes.

150 ml/¼ pint milk
100 g/4 oz whole unblanched almonds
15 ml/1 tbsp liquid honey
225 g/8 oz caster sugar
grated rind of 1 lemon
1 (700 ml/24 fl oz) bottle Irish whiskey
150 ml/¼ pint single cream

Combine the milk, almonds and honey in a saucepan. Bring to the boil, remove from the heat, cover and leave to stand until quite cold.

Strain the milk into a jug. Grind the almonds remaining in the strainer in a nut mill or food processor, or pound in a mortar with a pestle.

Transfer the ground almonds to a bowl and stir in the sugar. Add the lemon rind and whiskey, then stir in the cold milk and honey mixture. Add the cream. Pour into a large jar, close tightly and store for 10 days, shaking daily.

Pour the mixture through a filter paper into a large jug. Fill small bottles, corking them tightly. Store in a cool, dry place.

MAKES ABOUT 900 ML/1½ PINTS

ORANGE BRANDY

ILLUSTRATED ON PAGE 135

175 g/6 oz sugar lumps
2 oranges
1 (680 ml/23 fl oz) bottle of brandy

Rub a few of the sugar lumps over the oranges to absorb the oil. Put them in a large bowl with the remaining sugar lumps.

Pare the orange peel in thin strips, taking care to avoid the pith, and add to the bowl. Squeeze the oranges and strain the juice into the bowl. Crush the sugar cubes with a spoon. Stir in the brandy. Pour into a large jar, close tightly and set aside for 3 days, stirring several times a day.

When all the sugar has dissolved, strain the mixture into clean bottles. Cork tightly and store in a cool, dry place. The flavour will improve on keeping; preferably store for 1 year before opening.

MAKES ABOUT 1 LITRE/1¾ PINTS

CHERRY BRANDY

Morello cherries are bitter cherries which are used in cooking rather than for eating raw. These red fruit are used when only just ripe, when they contribute an excellent flavour.

450 g/1 lb morello cherries
75 g/3 oz sugar · brandy

Place the cherries in perfectly clean jars, sprinkling the sugar between the fruit. The jars should be full but not tightly packed. Top up with brandy to completely cover the cherries. Cover with airtight lids and invert each jar several times to dissolve the sugar. Store in a cool, dark place for 2-3 months before using. The cherries and liquor will keep for at least a year - years, according to Mrs Beeton.

GINGER WINE

All the rules which apply to home wine-making must be adopted when preparing this recipe: all equipment must be sterilized using a commercial sterilizing agent and air must be excluded from the wine at all stages in the fermentation and clearing process. Use Campden tablets or a suitable product for arresting the fermentation, then add wine finings to clear the wine or filter it until clear. The bottles and corks must also be sterilized. The quantities given here are only a proportion of those in the original recipe which called for nine gallons of water. The original method was far simpler, based on fermenting the wine in a cask for a fortnight, then adding the brandy and corking down the cask by degrees. Then the wine was left for a few weeks before bottling. If you have a cold cellar or outhouse, you may like to experiment with the old-fashioned method; however, the recipe below is likely to give more reliable results.

pared rind and juice of 1 lemon
50 g/2 oz fresh root ginger
1.4 kg/3 lb sugar
1 sachet of wine yeast
100 g/4 oz raisins, chopped
Campden tablets
wine finings or filter
300 ml/½ pint brandy

Place the lemon rind in a large saucepan. Cut the ginger in half and hit both pieces with a meat mallet or rolling pin, then add them to the pan with 450 g/1 lb sugar and 1.1 litres/2 pints water. Stir until the sugar has dissolved, then bring to the boil and cook for 5 minutes. Skim off any scum which rises to the surface of the syrup.

Pour the syrup into a sterilized fermentation bucket and add 1.1 litres/2 pints cold water. Stir in the yeast, cover the bucket and leave in a warm place overnight. Next day, stir in another 450 g/1 lb sugar, the strained lemon juice and another 1.1 litres/2 pints water. Divide the raisins equally between two sterilized fermentation jars. Add a piece of ginger and half the lemon rind from the wine to each jar, then stir the liquid well to ensure that all the sugar has dissolved and divide it between the jars. Fit airlocks on the jars and leave them in a warm place.

When the initial fierce fermentation has subsided (about 3 days), place the remaining sugar in a saucepan with 1.1 litres/2 pints water and bring to the boil, stirring until the sugar has dissolved completely. Leave to cool, then divide the syrup equally between the two jars of wine. Leave until the wine has finished fermenting - about 2 weeks. Shake the jars every day during this period.

Leave the wine for a day, then siphon it into clean jars, leaving the sediment. Add 1-2 dissolved Campden tablets to each jar, cover with an airlock and leave in a cold place for 1-2 days, until the wine settles and forms a sediment. Siphon off the wine from the sediment, add finings, then filter it. Add the brandy. Bottle, cork and label the wine. Store it in a cold, dark place for at least 4-6 weeks.

MAKES ABOUT 6.8 LITRES/1 ½ GALLONS

WELSH NECTAR

With a flavour reminiscent of grape juice, Welsh Nectar is a pleasant alcohol-free drink. Those who find it rather sweet may prefer to dilute it with soda water or spring water.

2 lemons
225 g/8 oz sugar lumps, crushed
225 g/8 oz seedless raisins, minced or finely chopped

Pare the lemons thinly, taking care to avoid the pith. Put the peel in a large heatproof bowl. Add the sugar. Pour over 2.25 litres/4 pints boiling water. Stir until all the sugar has dissolved. Cover and leave to cool.

Squeeze the lemons; strain the juice into the bowl. Stir in the raisins. Pour into a large jar, close tightly and set aside for 4-5 days, stirring several times a day. Strain the mixture through a jelly bag into clean bottles. Cover and refrigerate. Use within 2 weeks.

MAKES ABOUT 2 LITRES/3½ PINTS

𝒮LOE GIN

450 g/1 lb ripe sloes
225 g/8 oz caster sugar
1 litre/1¾ pints dry gin

Remove stalks and leaves from the sloes, then wash and prick them all over. Put them in a jar which can be fitted with an airtight seal.

In a large jug or bowl, dissolve the sugar in the gin and pour it on to the sloes. Cover the jar and store it in a cool dark place for 3 months, giving it a gentle shake every few days to extract and distribute the fruit flavour. Strain, bottle and store for about 3 months more before serving.

MAKES ABOUT 1.25 LITRES/2¼ PINTS

𝒜LCOHOL-FREE PUNCH

300 g/11 oz caster sugar
150 ml/¼ pint strong black tea
250ml/8 floz lemon juice
350 ml/12 fl oz orange juice
1 litre/1¾ pints white grape juice
1 (227 g/8 oz) can crushed pineapple
2 litres/3½ pints ginger ale
ice cubes
1 (170 g/6 oz) bottle maraschino cherries, drained
2 lemons, sliced
2 oranges, sliced

Put the sugar in a large saucepan with 3.5 litres/6 pints water. Stir over gentle heat until the sugar has dissolved, then boil for 6 minutes. Stir in the tea and set aside until cool. Pour into one or two large jugs or bowls; cover and chill.

When quite cold, add the fruit juices and crushed pineapple. Just before serving, pour in the ginger ale and add the ice cubes. Add the maraschino cherries, stir once; float the citrus slices on top.

SERVES ABOUT 48

𝒪RANGE SQUASH

Campden tablets, available from chemists and shops specializing in wine-making equipment, consist of sodium metabisulphite. They are used for killing off wild yeasts in fruit when making wine. Adding a Campden tablet to this squash prevents the orange juice from fermenting.

grated rind of 3 oranges
450 g/1 lb sugar
¼ lemon, cut in wedges
300 ml/½ pint fresh orange juice
1 Campden tablet

Combine the orange rind, sugar and lemon wedges in a saucepan. Add 450 ml/¾ pint water and heat gently, stirring to dissolve the sugar, until boiling. Leave over low heat for 30 minutes, then set aside until cold.

Add the orange juice, stir and strain into a clean jug. Squeeze, then discard the lemon wedges in the strainer. Crush the Campden tablet in a mug and add a little boiling water. Stir until dissolved, then add to the squash. Stir well before pouring into a bottle. Cover and store in the refrigerator for up to 3 weeks. To serve, dilute to taste with water, soda water or mineral water.

MAKES ABOUT 1 LITRE/1¾ PINTS

ℒEMONADE

A jug of lemonade always goes down well with young guests. Served with carbonated spring water it proves popular with drivers.

1.8 kg/4 lb sugar
grated rind of 2 lemons
1 litre/1¾ pints lemon juice

Put the sugar in a saucepan with 1 litre/1¾ pints water. Heat gently, stirring until all the sugar has dissolved, then stir in the lemon rind. Boil for 5 minutes without further stirring. Cool. Stir in the lemon juice, strain into clean jugs or bottles and store in the refrigerator. Dilute with iced water to serve.

MAKES ABOUT 3 LITRES/5¼ PINTS

MENUS FOR THE FESTIVE SEASON

Drinks Party

Holding a drinks party is an excellent way of launching the festive season and it provides the perfect opportunity for friends, distant relatives and neighbours to exchange greetings and gifts, if appropriate, before everyone goes their separate ways for the Christmas holiday.

TIMING

The party may be planned for lunchtime or early evening, or you may decide to make it an 'open house' if you intend inviting a large number of guests. Opting for the latter is a good way of seeing friends with children, who may arrive at lunchtime or in the afternoon, as well as elderly relatives, single guests and couples. Most people have multiple commitments and a dozen things to do over the weekends running up to Christmas, so if you can afford the time this would doubtless prove a popular choice.

INVITATIONS

Remember that everyone gets booked up early over Christmas, so send out written invitations at least a couple of weeks in advance, if not sooner. Telephone invitations are quite acceptable for informal gatherings - but it is a good idea to send a note confirming the date and time.

PLANNING AND ORGANISING THE PARTY

The first stage in planning a drinks party is the drawing up of the guest list, deciding on the date and time. This will give you have a clear idea of the work involved. Next, decide on the drinks and food before thinking about other domestic details, such as how best to arrange the room for the party.

DRINKS

If you invite a small number of guests, you may decide to offer a variety of drinks, including sherry, spirits, aperitifs, wine, beers and soft drinks. However, the more practical approach is to limit the selection to red and white wine, and soft drinks. A bowl of mulled wine is ideal and makes a welcoming drink on cold days. Always provide plenty of mineral water, mixers (if appropriate), fruit juice and low-alcohol or alcohol-free beers.

FOOD

Provide a variety of bought snacks, such as nuts, olives, breadsticks and savoury biscuits. Keep the food simple and easy to eat - dips, crudités and sweet and savoury pastries are all suitable. The suggested menu is perfect for the Christmas period, when guests appreciate seasonal bakes, such as mince pies. Mince pies and sausage rolls can be made and frozen uncooked well ahead, ready for baking on the morning of the party or the day before. Display the food attractively on large platters or trays which can be handed around easily. It is also a good idea to have a small table laid with the food and to include a neat stack of paper napkins and small plates.

ARRANGING THE ROOM

The party may be held in one or more rooms according to numbers and space. Clear furniture to the sides of the room if you expect large numbers but try to avoid making the area look like a dentist's waiting room by distributing chairs to other areas or stacking them away in a bedroom until after the party. Do keep a few seats in the room for those who prefer not to stand. It is important to have plenty of surfaces on which to stand drinks and to protect precious furniture – drink mats are more practical than

cloths which can be pulled off easily by accident in a crowded room. If any of the guests are likely to smoke, make sure that there are plenty of ash trays available.

GREETING GUESTS

To make sure you have space for guests' coats, clear hall cupboards or coat stands before a small gathering. If you expect a larger number of guests it is a good idea to set aside a bedroom for coats. Greet guests on arrival and offer them a drink, then introduce them to other guests and open the conversation. Be ready to rescue any who are left out of the party by drawing them into a group of people.

SAYING GOODBYE

Seeing off guests is almost as important as greeting them. If you are holding a large party, make sure guests know where their coats are so that you do not have to attend to them individually as they leave; however, do be aware of people who may be seeking you out to say farewell. It is not difficult to make partings brief at this time of year, when an exchange of season's greetings is quite sufficient, and this avoids breaking up the party.

> *'When any of the carriages of the guests are announced, or the time for their departure arrived, they should make a slight intimation to the hostess, without, however, exciting any observation, that they are about to depart. If this cannot be done, however, without creating too much bustle, it will be better for the visitors to retire quietly without taking their leave.'*
>
> MRS BEETON (1861)

MRS BEETON'S PASTRY RAMAKINS

These cheese savouries can be made with the odd pieces of cheese left from a cheeseboard. Mix a little strong cheese with any mild-flavoured leftovers.

oil for greasing
225 g/8 oz fresh or thawed frozen puff pastry
175 g/6 oz Stilton or Cheshire cheese, or a mixture of Parmesan and mild cheese, grated or finely crumbled
1 egg yolk

Grease a baking sheet. Set the oven at 220°C/425°F/gas 7. Roll out the pastry into an oblong measuring about 20 x 10 cm/8 x 4 inches. Sprinkle half the cheese over the middle of the pastry. Fold the bottom third over the cheese, then fold the top third down. Give the pastry a quarter turn clockwise, then roll it out into an oblong about the same size as the original shape.

Sprinkle the remaining cheese over the pastry and repeat the folding and rolling. Finally, roll out the pastry to about 2.5 mm/⅛ inch thick, or slightly thicker. Use fancy cutters to stamp out shapes - fluted circles, diamonds, triangles or crescents - and place them on the baking sheet. Stir 5 ml/1 tsp water into the egg and brush it over the pastries. Bake for 10-15 minutes, until puffed and browned. Serve freshly baked.

MAKES ABOUT 24

A Merry Christmas and a Happy New Year.

SAUSAGE ROLLS

400 g/14 oz fresh or thawed frozen puff pastry
flour for rolling out
400 g/14 oz sausagemeat
1 egg yolk, beaten

Set the oven at 230°C/450°F/gas 8. On a lightly floured surface roll out the pastry thinly to a large rectangle. Cut the rectangle in half lengthways. Divide the sausagemeat in half and form each half into a long thin roll, the same length as the pastry. Place one roll of sausage on a strip of pastry, bring the pastry over to enclose it and seal the joins with egg yolk. Make the second long roll in the same way.

Cut each long sausage roll neatly into 5 cm/2 inch slices. Arrange the sausage rolls on ungreased baking sheets, making sure that the joins are underneath. Glaze with the remaining egg yolk.

Bake the sausage rolls for 10 minutes, or until the pastry is well risen and brown. Reduce the oven temperature to 180°C/350°F/gas 4, and continue baking for 20-25 minutes. Cover the sausage rolls loosely with foil if the pastry overbrowns.

MAKES ABOUT 24

BURLINGTON CROUTES

100 g/4 oz cooked chicken, finely chopped
30 ml/2 tbsp mayonnaise
2 tomatoes, each cut into 6 thin slices
salt and pepper
12 rounds of fried bread or crackers
butter (optional) · 12 stuffed olives

Mix the chicken with the mayonnaise. Sprinkle tomato slices with salt and pepper. If using fried bread, drain thoroughly on absorbent kitchen paper. Butter crackers, if using. Place a slice of tomato on each bread round or cracker. Pile the chicken mixture on top. Top each croûte with a stuffed olive.

MAKES TWELVE

AUBERGINE DIP

Aubergine shells are used as containers for this richly-flavoured dip.

2 small aubergines
75 ml/3 fl oz olive oil
1 large onion, finely chopped
2 garlic cloves, crushed
100 g/4 oz mushrooms, chopped
1 small green pepper, seeded and chopped
1 (397 g/14 oz) can chopped tomatoes with herbs, sieved or puréed
250 ml/8 fl oz tomato juice
15 ml/1 tbsp red wine vinegar
5 ml/1 tsp caster sugar
salt and pepper

Cut the aubergines in half lengthways. Scoop out the flesh, leaving the shells intact. Pack the shells on top of each other. Wrap closely in cling film. Refrigerate until required.

Make the dip. Cube the aubergine flesh. Heat the oil in a large frying pan. Add the onion and aubergine and fry for 5 minutes over moderate heat. Stir in the garlic, mushrooms and green pepper. Stir fry for 5 minutes.

Purée the chopped tomatoes, with their juices, in a blender or food processor. Alternatively, press them through a sieve into a bowl. Add the tomato purée to the pan with the tomato juice, vinegar and sugar. Bring to the boil, lower the heat and simmer, uncovered, for 20-30 minutes, stirring occasionally. Add salt and pepper to taste. When the mixture is very thick, remove it from the heat. Cool, then chill until required.

To serve, unwrap the aubergine shells and arrange them on a serving platter. Fill each shell with the aubergine mixture, piling it up in the centre. Serve with Melba toast, crackers or French bread.

SERVES EIGHT

Pâté Maison (page 65),
for slicing, with Potted Mushrooms
(page 65) and Potted Ham (page 41)

Hummus

Serve as a starter or snack, with French bread, pitta or crispbreads.

150 g/5 oz chick peas, soaked overnight or for several hours
in water to cover
1 garlic clove, chopped
salt
90 ml/6 tbsp olive oil
60 ml/4 tbsp tahini (bought or see Mrs Beeton's Tip)
60 ml/4 tbsp lemon juice
chopped parsley to garnish

Drain the chick peas, put them in a clean saucepan and add fresh water to cover. Bring to the boil, lower the heat and simmer for 1-1½ hours until very tender. Drain thoroughly, then mash and sieve or crush in a mortar with a pestle to a smooth paste. An alternative, and much easier method, is to process the chick peas in a blender or food processor.

Add the garlic and salt to taste. Stir briskly until well mixed, then gradually work in the olive oil, as when making mayonnaise. The chick peas should form a creamy paste. Work in the tahini slowly, adding it a teaspoonful at a time at first. When the mixture is creamy work in lemon juice to taste.

Transfer the hummus to a shallow serving bowl and sprinkle with chopped parsley.

SERVES SIX TO EIGHT

MRS BEETON'S TIP
To make tahini, mix 50 g/2 oz ground sesame seeds, 1 crushed garlic clove, 1.25 ml/¼ tsp salt, 15 ml/1 tbsp lemon juice and a pinch of pepper. Add 75 ml/5 tbsp water. Sieve to a smooth purée or process in a blender or food processor for a few minutes. Add more salt and pepper if required.

Mince Pies

ILLUSTRATED ON PAGES 7 AND 31

As a contrast to the more conventional mincemeat, fill these pies with the Lemon Mincemeat on page 14. The slightly tart flavour is particularly appropriate for serving with drinks.

350 g/12 oz mincemeat
25 g/1 oz caster sugar for dredging

SHORT CRUST PASTRY
300 g/10 oz plain flour
5 ml/1 tsp salt
150 g/5 oz margarine (or half butter, half lard)
flour for rolling out

Set the oven at 200℃/400℉/gas 6. To make the pastry, sift the flour and salt into a bowl, then rub in the margarine until the mixture resembles fine breadcrumbs. Add enough cold water to make a stiff dough. Press the dough together with your fingertips.

Roll out the pastry on a lightly floured surface and use just over half of it to line twelve 7.5 cm/3 inch patty tins. Cut out 12 lids from the rest of the pastry. If liked, make holly leaf decorations from the pastry trimmings.

Place a spoonful of mincemeat in each pastry case. Dampen the edges of the cases and cover with the pastry lids. Seal the edges well. Brush the tops with water and add any pastry decorations. Dredge with the sugar. Make 2 small cuts in the top of each pie. Bake for 15-20 minutes or until golden brown.

MAKES TWELVE

MRS BEETON'S TIP
Festive mince pies can also be made using flaky, rough puff or puff pastry with mouthwatering results. If using any of these pastries you will require 200 g/7 oz flour.

Breakfast Buffet

Entertaining early in the day can be fun between Christmas and the New Year when friends are on holiday, or on a weekend before the festivities get underway. A traditional British breakfast buffet can easily be adapted to suit any number of guests, with cook-ahead food for large numbers and a few last-minute dishes for small gatherings.

FRUIT AND CEREALS

A splendid array of fresh fruit makes an excellent centrepiece for a breakfast buffet. It is also a good idea to set out a selection of dried fruits and shelled nuts, such as apricots, raisins, sultanas, walnuts, brazils and hazelnuts. Cereals may not seem exceptionally exciting; however, a large bowl of home-made muesli and another of Greek yogurt makes a tempting first course when served with fresh fruit such as bananas.

COLD PLATTERS

Kipper mousse is a simple, prepare-ahead alternative to grilled kippers which are not practical for buffets. Include an array of cold meats and sliced cheese to provide alternatives for all tastes and add a couple of simple salads, such as tomato or potato salad.

HOT DISHES

Crisp, golden fried potatoes tempt the most reluctant of breakfast diners into sampling a hot meal early in the day. As well as a steaming bowl of kedgeree, which is easy to prepare in a large quantity, provide chipolata sausages, bacon rolls and a dish of sliced black pudding. When preparing large quantities, all of these may be baked in a hot oven instead of frying or grilling which demands constant attention. Lastly, a tureen of steaming-hot, creamy scrambled eggs can be prepared without too much effort for small and medium-sized gatherings.

ASIDES AND DRINKS

Croissants and home-made jam will appeal to those who do not want to eat a large meal. Toasted muffins are delicious with a little marmalade to round off a traditional hot breakfast. Warm bread rolls, soda bread or rye crispbread may also be served.

Buck's Fizz (sparkling white wine or champagne with orange juice) or plain champagne always gets a breakfast off to a good start but you should also have plenty of freshly-squeezed orange juice, mineral water, tea and coffee. Making tea for a crowd can be extremely time-consuming, so try offering a variety of fruit or herb tea bags instead. Arrange them in a basket in the kitchen and ask guests to help themselves, adding their own boiling water.

*P*OTTED HAM

ILLUSTRATED ON PAGE 39

butter for greasing
1.25 kg/2¾ lb cooked ham, not too lean
1.25 ml/¼ tsp ground mace
1.25 ml/¼ tsp grated nutmeg
pinch of cayenne pepper
1.25 ml/¼ tsp ground black pepper
melted clarified butter (see Mrs Beeton's Tip, page 65)

Grease a pie dish. Set the oven at 180°C/350°F/gas 4. Mince the ham two or three times, then pound well and rub through a fine sieve into a clean bowl. Add the spices and peppers and mix well. Spoon the ham mixture into the prepared pie dish, cover with buttered greaseproof paper and bake for about 45 minutes.

When cooked, allow to cool, then turn into small pots and cover with clarified butter. Refrigerate until the butter is firm.

MAKES ABOUT 1 KG/2¼ LB

KIPPER MOUSSE

fat for greasing
75 g/3 oz butter
3 mushrooms, chopped
6 black peppercorns
12 parsley stalks
25 g/1 oz plain flour
250 ml/8 fl oz fish stock (see Mrs Beeton's Tip, page 48) or chicken stock
salt and pepper
lemon juice
1 small onion, finely sliced
575 g/1¼ lb kipper fillets, skinned and cut into 2.5 cm/1 inch pieces
250 ml/8 fl oz mayonnaise
75 ml/5 tbsp dry white wine
15 g/½ oz gelatine
250 ml/8 fl oz double cream

GARNISH
lemon slices
parsley sprigs

Melt 25 g/1 oz of the butter in a saucepan; add the chopped mushrooms, peppercorns and parsley stalks. Cook over gentle heat for 10 minutes. Add the flour and stir over low heat for 2-3 minutes, without allowing the mixture to colour. Gradually add the stock and simmer, stirring, for 3-4 minutes. Rub the sauce through a sieve into a clean saucepan. Add salt, pepper and lemon juice to taste. Cover the saucepan closely and set aside until cold.

Grease a soufflé dish or oval pâté mould. Melt the remaining butter in a frying pan, add the onion and fry gently for 2-3 minutes. Add the fish and fry gently for 7 minutes more. Tip the contents of the pan into a large bowl and stir in the cold sauce and the mayonnaise. Process the mixture in a blender or food processor or pound to a smooth paste in a mortar. Using a rubber spatula, scrape the purée into a large bowl.

Place the wine in a small bowl and sprinkle the gelatine on to the liquid. Set aside for 15 minutes until the gelatine is spongy. Stand the bowl over a saucepan of hot water and stir the gelatine until it has dissolved completely. Add it to the kipper purée and mix very thoroughly. Blend in the cream and add salt, pepper and a dash of lemon juice to taste.

Turn the mixture into the prepared dish or mould, cover the surface closely and chill for at least 2 hours. Serve from the dish or turn out on to a serving dish. Garnish with lemon slices and parsley sprigs.

SERVES EIGHT AS PART OF A BUFFET

FRIED KIDNEYS

Per portion:
2 lamb's kidneys
15-25 g/½-1 oz butter
salt and pepper
1 slice toast

Remove any fat and skin surrounding the kidneys, then slice them in half, leaving the two pieces attached so that each kidney can be opened out flat. Snip out the cores of the kidneys, then season them well.

Melt 15 g/½ oz of the butter in a frying pan. Add the kidneys, flat-side down, and fry over moderate heat for 7-8 minutes or until firm and cooked through. Turn the kidneys halfway through cooking. Serve the kidneys on hot, dry toast, with the pan juices poured over. Top with a little extra butter, if liked, and serve at once.

𝒦EDGEREE

ILLUSTRATED ON PAGE 51

No Victorian country-house breakfast buffet would have been complete without kedgeree. Hard-boiled egg and parsley are the traditional garnish, sometimes arranged in the shape of the cross of St Andrew.

salt and pepper
150 g/5 oz long-grain rice
125 ml/4 fl oz milk
450 g/1 lb smoked haddock
50 g/2 oz butter
15 ml/1 tbsp curry powder
2 hard-boiled eggs, roughly chopped
cayenne pepper

GARNISH
15 g/½ oz butter
1 hard-boiled egg, white and yolk sieved separately
15 ml/1 tbsp chopped parsley

Bring a saucepan of salted water to the boil. Add the rice and cook for 12 minutes. Drain thoroughly, rinse under cold water and drain again. Place the strainer over a saucepan of simmering water to keep the rice warm.

Put the milk in a large shallow saucepan or frying pan with 125 ml/4 fl oz water. Bring to simmering point, add the fish and poach gently for 4 minutes. Using a slotted spoon and a fish slice, transfer the haddock to a wooden board. Discard the cooking liquid.

Remove the skin and any bones from the haddock and break up the flesh into fairly large flakes. Melt half the butter in a large saucepan. Blend in the curry powder and add the flaked fish. Warm the mixture through. Remove from the heat, lightly stir in the chopped eggs; add salt, pepper and cayenne.

Melt the remaining butter in a second pan, add the rice and toss until well coated. Add salt, pepper and cayenne. Add the rice to the haddock mixture and mix well. Pile the kedgeree on to a warmed dish.

Dot the kedgeree with the butter, garnish with sieved hard-boiled egg yolk, egg white and parsley and serve at once.

SERVES FOUR TO SIX AS PART OF A BUFFET

𝒦IDNEYS TURBIGO

15 ml/1 tbsp oil
225 g/8 oz cocktail sausages
1 small onion, finely chopped
450 g/1 lb lambs' kidneys, halved and cored
salt and pepper
100 g/4 oz small button mushrooms
15 ml/1 tbsp plain flour
30 ml/2 tbsp tomato purée
150 ml/¼ pint dry white wine
150 ml/¼ pint vegetable or chicken stock
45 ml/3 tbsp chopped parsley

Heat the oil in a large frying pan, add the sausages and cook them over moderate heat until evenly golden. Using a slotted spoon, transfer them to a dish and set aside.

Pour off any excess fat from the pan, leaving enough to cook the remaining ingredients. Add the onion and cook, stirring, for 10 minutes, until softened. Add the kidneys, with salt and pepper to taste. Cook them, turning often, until browned all over and just cooked.

Add the mushrooms to the pan and continue cooking for about 5 minutes, so that the mushrooms are lightly cooked. Use a slotted spoon to transfer the kidneys and mushrooms to the dish with the sausages.

Stir the flour into the fat remaining in the pan. Stir in the tomato purée, then gradually stir in the wine and stock. Bring to the boil, stirring all the time, then lower the heat and return the sausages, mushrooms and kidneys to the pan. Simmer gently for 5 minutes.

Add the parsley and seasoning to taste before serving with cooked pasta or rice.

SERVES FOUR TO SIX AS PART OF A BUFFET

PRESSED TONGUE

1 fresh ox tongue
1 onion, chopped
1 carrot, diced
1 turnip, diced
1 celery stick, sliced
1 bouquet garni
6 whole allspice
4 whole cloves
6 black peppercorns
chopped parsley to garnish

Weigh the tongue, then wash thoroughly. Soak in cold water for 2 hours. Drain and put in a large saucepan. Cover with fresh cold water, bring to the boil, then drain again. Repeat the process.

Return the tongue to the pan again, cover with cold water once more and add the vegetables, bouquet garni and spices. Bring to the boil, cover with a tight-fitting lid, lower the heat and simmer gently for about 3 hours (see Mrs Beeton's Tip).

When cooked, lift out the tongue and plunge into cold water. Drain. Remove the skin carefully and take out the small bones at the root of the tongue, together with any excess fat, glands and gristle. Curl the hot tongue into an 18 cm/7 inch straight-sided dish or tin. Spoon over a little of the hot stock in which the tongue was cooked, to fill up the crevices. Put a flat plate, just large enough to fit inside the dish, on top of the tongue, and add a heavy weight. Cool, then chill overnight until set. Run a knife around the tongue to loosen it from the container and turn it out. Cut into thin slices to serve.

SERVES NINE TO TWELVE

MRS BEETON'S TIP
To test whether the tongue is cooked, attempt to pull out one of the small bones near the root. If it comes away easily, the tongue is ready.

BACON ROLLS

To make bacon rolls, roll up bacon rashers loosely. Thread them in pairs on short metal skewers. Grill under moderately high heat for about 5 minutes, turning frequently, until the rolls are crisp. Alternatively, cook the rolls in a preheated 180°C/350°F/gas 4 oven for about 30 minutes.

ENGLISH MUFFINS

Serve the muffins split and toasted.

400 g/14 oz strong white flour
5 ml/1 tsp salt
25 g/1 oz butter or margarine
225 ml/7½ fl oz milk
10 ml/2 tsp dried yeast
1 egg · fat for frying

Sift the flour and salt into a large bowl. Rub in the butter or margarine. Place the milk in a saucepan and warm gently. It should be just hand-hot. Pour the milk into a small bowl, sprinkle the dried yeast on top and leave until frothy. Beat in the egg. Add the yeast liquid to the flour to make a very soft dough. Beat the dough by hand or with a wooden spoon for about 5 minutes until smooth and shiny. Cover the bowl with a large lightly oiled polythene bag and leave in a warm place for 1-2 hours or until doubled in bulk. Beat again lightly.

Roll out on a well floured surface to a thickness of about 1 cm/½ inch. Using a plain 7.5 cm/3 inch cutter, cut the dough into rounds. Place the rounds on a floured baking sheet, cover with polythene and leave to rise for about 45 minutes. Heat a griddle or heavy-bottomed frying pan, then grease it. Cook the muffins on both sides for about 8 minutes until golden.

MAKES TWENTY

CROISSANTS

Rich, flaky French croissants make the perfect addition to a breakfast buffet, especially when home-made.

fat for greasing
400 g/14 oz strong white flour
5 ml/ 1 tsp salt
75 g/3 oz lard
25 g/1 oz fresh yeast or 15 ml/1 tbsp dried yeast
2.5 ml/½ tsp sugar
1 egg, beaten
flour for kneading
100 g/4 oz unsalted butter
beaten egg for glazing

Grease the baking sheet. Sift the flour and salt into a large bowl. Rub in 25 g/1 oz of the lard. Measure 200 ml/7 fl oz lukewarm water.

Blend the fresh yeast to a thin paste with the sugar and a little of the warm water. Set aside in a warm place until frothy – about 5 minutes. Alternatively, sprinkle the dried yeast over all the warm water and set aside until frothy, then stir well.

Stir the egg, yeast liquid and remaining water into the flour and mix to a soft dough. Turn on to a lightly floured surface and knead for about 8 minutes or until the dough is smooth and no longer sticky. Return the dough to the bowl and cover with cling film. Leave at room temperature for 15 minutes.

Meanwhile, roughly chop the remaining lard and the butter together until well mixed; then chill. On a lightly floured surface, roll out the dough into an oblong 50 x 20 cm/ 30 x 8 inches. Divide the chilled fat into three. Dot one-third over the top two-thirds of the dough, leaving a small border. Fold the dough into three by bringing the bottom third up and the top third down. Seal the edges by pressing with the rolling pin. Give the dough a quarter turn and repeat the rolling and folding twice, using the other two portions of the fat. Place the dough in a large, lightly oiled polythene bag. Leave in a cool place for 15 minutes.

Repeat the rolling and folding three more times. Rest the dough in the polythene bag for 15 minutes. Roll out to an oblong 34 x 23 cm/14 x 9 inches; cut into six 13 cm/5 inch squares. Cut each square into triangles. Brush the surface of the dough with beaten egg and roll each triangle loosely, towards the point, finishing with the tip underneath. Curve into a crescent shape. Place on the prepared baking sheet and brush with beaten egg. Place the baking sheet in the polythene bag again. Leave at room temperature for about 1 hour or until the dough is light and puffy. Set the oven at 220℃/425°F/gas 7.

Bake for 15-20 minutes, until golden brown and crisp. Cool on a wire rack.

MAKES TWELVE

IRISH SODA BREAD

fat for greasing
575 g/1¼ lb plain flour
5 ml/1 tsp bicarbonate of soda
5 ml/1 tsp salt
5 ml/1 tsp cream of tartar (if using fresh milk)
300 ml/½ pint buttermilk or soured milk or fresh milk
flour for dusting

Grease a baking sheet. Set the oven at 190-200℃/375-400°F/gas 5-6. Mix all the dry ingredients in a bowl, then make a well in the centre. Add enough milk to make a fairly slack dough, pouring it in almost all at once, not spoonful by spoonful. Mix with a wooden spoon, lightly and quickly.

With floured hands, place the mixture on a lightly floured surface and flatten the dough into a round about 2.5 cm/1 inch thick. Turn on to the prepared baking sheet. Make a large cross in the surface with a floured knife to make it heat through evenly.

Bake for about 40 minutes. Pierce the centre with a thin skewer to test for readiness; it should come out clean. Wrap the loaf in a clean tea-towel to keep it soft until required.

MAKES ONE 750 G/1¼ LB LOAF

MRS BEETON'S ORANGE SALAD

5 oranges
50 g/2 oz caster sugar (or to taste)
2.5 ml/½ tsp ground mixed spice
100 g/4 oz muscatel raisins
60 ml/4 tbsp brandy

Peel four oranges, removing all pith. Slice them, discarding the pips. Mix the sugar and spice in a bowl. Layer the orange slices in a serving dish, sprinkling each layer with the sugar mixture and raisins.

Squeeze the juice from the remaining orange and sprinkle it over the salad. Pour the brandy over, cover and macerate for 24 hours before serving.

SERVES EIGHT AS PART OF A BUFFET

DRIED FRUIT COMPOTE

100 g/4 oz dried apricots
100 g/4 oz prunes
100 g/4 oz dried figs
50 g/2 oz dried apple rings
30 ml/2 tbsp liquid honey
2.5 cm/1 inch cinnamon stick
2 cloves
pared rind and juice of lemon
50 g/2 oz raisins
50 g/2 oz flaked almonds, toasted

Combine the apricots, prunes and figs in a bowl. Add water to cover and leave to soak. Put the apples in a separate bowl with water to cover and leave both bowls to soak overnight.

Next day, place the honey in a saucepan with 600 ml/1 pint water. Add the cinnamon stick, cloves and lemon rind. Bring to the boil. Stir in the lemon juice.

Drain both bowls of soaked fruit. Add the mixed fruit to the pan, cover and simmer for 10 minutes. Stir in the drained apples and simmer for 10 minutes more, then add the raisins and simmer for 2-3 minutes. Discard the cinnamon, cloves and lemon rind.

Spoon the compote into a serving dish and sprinkle with the almonds. Serve warm or cold.

SERVES SIX

Tidings of Comfort and Joy.

MICROWAVE TIP

There is no need to presoak the dried fruit. Make the honey syrup in a large bowl, using 450 ml/¾ pint water. Microwave on High for about 4 minutes, then stir in all the dried fruit with the cinnamon, cloves and lemon rind. Cover and cook on High for 15-20 minutes or until all the fruit is soft. Stir several times during cooking, each time pressing the fruit down into the syrup.

Lunch Party

MENU
Consommé Jardinière

Tweed Kettle
with
Petits Pois à la française
Creamed Spinach
Small Baked Potatoes

Pears in Port Wine

CONSOMME JARDINIERE

100 g/4 oz shin of beef
1 small onion
1 small carrot
1 small celery stick
1.1 litres/2 pints cold brown stock
1 bouquet garni
salt
4 white peppercorns
white and crushed shell of 1 egg

GARNISH
15 ml/1 tbsp finely diced turnip
15 ml/1 tbsp finely diced carrot
15 ml/1 tbsp small green peas
15 ml/1 tbsp tiny cauliflower florets or 15 ml/1 tbsp finely
diced cucumber

Shred the beef finely, trimming off all the fat. Transfer it to a bowl, add 125 ml/4 fl oz water and soak for 15 minutes. Tip the contents of the bowl into a large saucepan. Stir in the remaining ingredients, adding the egg white and shell last. Heat slowly to simmering point, whisking constantly, until a froth rises to the surface. Remove the whisk, cover, and simmer the consommé very gently for 1½-2 hours. Do not allow it to boil or the froth will break up and cloud the consommé.

Strain slowly into a large bowl through muslin or a scalded jelly bag. If necessary, strain the consommé again. Pour the consommé into a clean saucepan. Adjust the seasoning. Reheat.

Meanwhile make the garnish by cooking the vegetables separately in boiling salted water until just tender. Drain and rinse the vegetables; then put them into a warmed tureen. Pour the hot consommé over the vegetables and serve.

SERVES SIX

CURLED BUTTER

'Tie a strong cloth by two of the corners to an iron hook in the wall; make a knot with the other two ends, so that a stick might pass through. Put the butter into the cloth; twist it tightly over a dish, into which the butter will fall through the knot, so forming small and pretty little strings. The butter may then be garnished with parsley, if to serve with a cheese course; or it may be sent to table plain for breakfast, in an ornamental dish. Squirted butter for garnishing hams, salads, eggs, etc., is made by forming a piece of stiff paper in the shape of a cornet, and squeezing the butter in fine strings from the hole at the bottom. Scooped butter is made by dipping a teaspoon or scooper in warm water, and then scooping the butter quickly and thin. In warm weather, it would not be necessary to heat the spoon.'

MRS BEETON (1861)

DINNER ROLLS

fat for greasing
800 g/1¾ lb strong white flour
10 ml/2 tsp sugar
400 ml/14 fl oz milk
25 g/1 oz fresh yeast or 15 ml/1 tbsp dried yeast
10 ml/2 tsp salt
50 g/2 oz butter or margarine
1 egg
flour for kneading
beaten egg for glazing

Grease two baking sheets. Sift about 75 g/3 oz of the flour and all the sugar into a large bowl. Warm the milk until lukewarm, then blend in the fresh yeast or stir in the dried yeast. Pour the yeast liquid into the flour and sugar and beat well. Leave the bowl in a warm place for 20 minutes.

Sift the remaining flour and the salt into a bowl. Rub in the butter or margarine. Beat the egg into the yeast mixture and stir in the flour mixture. Mix to a soft dough. Turn on to a lightly floured surface and knead for about 5 minutes or until the dough is smooth and no longer sticky. Return to the bowl and cover with cling film. Leave in a warm place until the dough has doubled in bulk - this will take up to 2 hours, or longer.

Knead the dough again until firm. Cut into 50 g/2 oz pieces, then shape each piece into a ball. Place on the prepared baking sheets 5-7.5 cm/2-3 inches apart. Brush with beaten egg. Cover with sheets of lightly oiled polythene. Leave in a warm place for about 20 minutes or until the rolls have doubled in bulk. Set the oven at 220°C/425°F/gas 7. Bake for 12-15 minutes until the rolls are golden brown.

MAKES 24

TWEED KETTLE

575 g/1¼ lb middle cut salmon
500 ml/17 fl oz fish stock (see Mrs Beeton's Tip)
250 ml/8 fl oz dry white wine
pinch of ground mace
salt and pepper
25 g/1 oz chopped shallots or snipped chives
5 ml/1 tsp chopped parsley
25 g/1 oz butter
30 ml/2 tbsp plain flour

Put the salmon in a saucepan with the fish stock, wine and mace. Add salt and pepper to taste. Bring the liquid to simmering point and simmer gently for 10-15 minutes or until the fish is just cooked through.

Using a slotted spoon and a fish slice, transfer the fish to a large plate. Remove the skin and bones and return them to the stock in the pan. Transfer the skinned fish to a warmed serving dish and keep hot.

Simmer the stock and fish trimmings for 10 minutes, then strain into a clean pan. Simmer gently, uncovered, until reduced by half. Stir in the shallots or chives and the parsley and remove from the heat.

In a small bowl, blend the butter with the flour. Gradually add small pieces of the mixture to the stock, whisking thoroughly after each addition. Return to the heat and simmer for 5 minutes, stirring. Pour the sauce over the fish and serve at once.

SERVES FOUR

MRS BEETON'S TIP
A simple fish stock can be made from fish bones and trimmings with 2-3 onion slices, 1 sliced celery stick, 2 white peppercorns, 1 bouquet garni and 600 ml/1 pint water. Bring the water to the boil, lower the heat and simmer for 30 minutes. Add salt to taste. Strain.

PETITS POIS A LA FRANCAIS

50 g/2 oz butter
1 lettuce heart, shredded
1 bunch of spring onions, finely chopped
675 g/1½ lb fresh shelled garden peas or frozen petits pois
pinch of sugar
salt and pepper

Melt the butter in a heavy-bottomed saucepan and add the lettuce, spring onions, peas and sugar, with salt and pepper to taste. Cover and simmer very gently until the peas are tender. Frozen petits pois may be ready in less than 10 minutes, but fresh garden peas could take 25 minutes.

SERVES SIX

CREAMED SPINACH

1 kg/2¼ lb spinach
50 g/2 oz butter
150 ml/5 fl oz single cream, scalded (see Mrs Beeton's Tip)
2.5 ml/½ tsp caster sugar
salt and pepper
grated nutmeg

Wash the fresh spinach several times and remove any coarse stalks. Put into a saucepan with just the water that clings to the leaves, then cover the pan. Put the pan over high heat for 2-3 minutes, shaking it frequently. Lower the heat, stir the spinach and cook for a further 2-3 minutes, turning the spinach occasionally until lightly cooked. Drain thoroughly, then chop the spinach coarsely.

Melt the butter in a large saucepan. Add the spinach. Stir lightly over gentle heat until most of the butter has been absorbed. Stir in the cream and sugar, with salt, pepper and nutmeg to taste. Heat through over low heat; serve at once.

SERVES FOUR

PEARS IN PORT

8 pears, peeled, cored and halved
150 g/5 oz sugar
6 cloves
6 allspice berries
150 ml/¼ pint port
cochineal or pink food colouring (optional)

Leave the stalks on the pear halves when preparing them. Lay the halves in a saucepan. Sprinkle the sugar over the fruit, add the cloves, allspice berries and 300 ml/½ pint water. Then add the port and bring the liquid to the boil, stirring to dissolve the sugar. Reduce the heat so that the syrup just simmers, cover the pan and simmer the fruit for about 20 minutes or until the pears are tender.

Transfer the pears to a serving dish. Boil the syrup until it is reduced by about half. Add a few drops of cochineal or pink food colouring, if liked, then pour the syrup over the pears. Leave to cool before serving.

SERVES FOUR TO EIGHT

> ### MRS BEETON'S TIP
> To scald cream, pour it into a saucepan and bring to just below boiling point over moderate heat. As soon as bubbles start to form around the rim of the milk, remove the pan from the heat.

A Buffet Party

MENU
Prawn Celeste
Lobster Salad

Raised Pheasant Pie
Mrs Beeton's Boiled Salad

Nesselrode Pudding
Meringues
Rich Chocolate Sauce

PRAWN CELESTE

100 g/4 oz butter
225 g/8 oz mushrooms, sliced
30 ml/2 tbsp plain flour
salt and pepper
250 ml/8 fl oz milk
250 ml/8 fl oz single cream
450 g/1 lb peeled cooked prawns
15 ml/1 tbsp dry sherry or to taste
chopped parsley, to garnish
8 slices of toast, cut in triangles, to serve

Melt the butter in a saucepan, add the mushrooms and cook over moderate heat for 3-4 minutes. Stir in the flour, with salt and pepper to taste and cook gently for 3 minutes.

Gradually add the milk and cream, stirring constantly until the sauce thickens. Add the prawns and sherry. Spoon into a warmed serving dish, garnish with the parsley and serve with the toast.

SERVES EIGHT

LOBSTER SALAD

2 cooked lobsters
75 ml/5 tbsp oil
30 ml/2 tbsp white wine vinegar
5 ml/1 tsp prepared mustard
2.5 ml/½ tsp anchovy essence
2 egg yolks
salt
pinch of cayenne pepper
pinch of caster sugar
1 endive, shredded
1 punnet of mustard and cress, snipped
2 celery sticks, chopped
¼ cucumber, thinly sliced
100 g/4 oz cooked beetroot, diced
2 eggs, hard-boiled

Twist off the lobster claws. Split the lobsters in half lengthways. Carefully remove the meat from the claws and body. Reserve any bright red coral or roe which may be found in a female (hen) lobster. Set aside the tail meat in large, neat pieces, then chop the remaining meat.

Combine the oil, vinegar, mustard, anchovy essence and egg yolks in a screw-top jar. Add a little salt, the cayenne pepper and sugar, then shake the mixture thoroughly until the ingredients combine to make a creamy dressing. Mix the endive, mustard and cress and celery in a large bowl. pour in the dressing and toss well. Mix in the chopped lobster meat, then transfer the salad to a large, shallow serving dish, scraping all the dressing from the bowl.

Cut the tail meat into neat pieces and arrange them on the salad. Arrange the cucumber and beetroot on the salad, setting the beetroot apart to avoid staining the cucumber and lobster. Use a teaspoon to scoop the yolks from the hard-boiled eggs, then rub them through a sieve. Chop the egg whites and arrange them on the salad. Finally add the sieved egg yolk and any reserved coral from the lobster.

SERVES SIX

Kedgeree (page 43) is a classic British breakfast dish which is ideal buffet fare

ℛAISED PHEASANT PIE

450 g/1 lb plain flour
2.5 ml/½ tsp salt
225 g/8 oz butter or margarine
2 egg yolks
1 hen pheasant, boned, carcass retained
grated nutmeg
1.25 ml/¼ tsp ground allspice
salt and pepper
2 quantities Mrs Beeton's Forcemeat (page 82)
2 veal escalopes
1 thick slice of cooked ham (about 50-75 g/2-3 oz)
beaten egg for glazing
1 small onion, quartered
1 bay leaf
1 carrot, quartered lengthways
10 ml/2 tsp gelatine

To make the pastry, mix the flour and salt in a large bowl. Add the butter or margarine and rub it into the flour until the mixture resembles fine breadcrumbs. Make a well in the middle and add the egg yolks with about 60 ml/4 tbsp water. Mix the pastry to a smooth, fairly soft dough, adding extra water as necessary. The pastry should have a little more water than ordinary short crust dough but it must not be sticky.

Set the oven at 160°C/325°F/gas 3. Grease a 23 cm/9 inch raised pie mould with a little oil and place it on a baking sheet. Set aside one-third of the pastry for the lid, then roll out the remainder into an oblong shape, about twice the size of the top of the mould. Do not be tempted to roll the pastry out into a sheet large enough to completely line the mould as it may break when you lift it into the mould. Carefully lift the pastry into the mould, then use the back of your fingers and knuckles to press it into the base of the mould, smoothing it up the sides to line the mould completely.

Open out the pheasant and sprinkle it with a little nutmeg, the allspice, salt and pepper. Set aside half the forcemeat, then divide the remainder into two portions. Spread one portion over the middle of the pheasant and lay the veal escalopes on top. Lay the cooked ham on top of the veal, then spread the second portion of forcemeat over the ham. Fold the sides of the boned pheasant around the stuffing.

Put half the reserved forcemeat into the base of the pie, particularly around the edges. Put the pheasant in the pie, placing the join in the skin downwards. Use the remaining forcemeat to fill in around the pheasant, packing it neatly into gaps.

Cut off a small piece of the remaining pastry and set it aside to make leaves for the pastry lid. Roll out the rest to a shape slightly larger than the top of the pie. Dampen the rim of the pastry lining with a little water, then lift the lid on top of the pie and press the edges to seal in the filling. Trim off any excess pastry. Pinch up the pastry edges. Roll out the trimmings with the reserved pastry and cut out leaves for the top of the pie. Cut a small hole to allow steam to escape, then glaze the pie with beaten egg.

Bake the pie for 3 hours. Check it frequently and cover it loosely with a piece of foil after the first hour to prevent the pastry from overcooking. Increase the oven temperature to 190°C/375°F/gas 5, uncover the pie and glaze it with a little more egg. Cook for a further 20-30 minutes, until the pastry is golden and glossy.

While the pie is cooking, simmer the pheasant carcass in a saucepan with the onion, bay leaf and carrot for 1½ hours. Make sure that there is plenty of water to cover the carcass and keep the pan covered. Strain the stock into a clean pan, then boil it hard, uncovered, until it is reduced to 300 ml/½ pint. Strain it through a muslin-lined sieve, then taste and season it.

When the pie is cooked, heat the stock and sprinkle gelatine into it. Remove the pan from the heat and stir until the gelatine has dissolved completely. Set this aside to cool. When the pie has cooled until it is just hot and the stock is cold, pour the stock slowly in through the vent in the top crust.

Cool the pie in the tin, then carefully remove the clips which hold the sides of the tin together; ease the sides away from the pie.

SERVES SIX TO EIGHT

Mrs Beeton's Boiled Salad

Halving the quantities given in the original recipe makes this workable for today's households. Chopped tarragon, chervil or burnet may be added to the salad.

1 head of celery, trimmed
1 small onion, chopped
½ cauliflower, broken into florets
350 g/12 oz French beans, trimmed
1 lettuce heart, shredded (optional)
125 ml/4 fl oz Mayonnaise (page 66), thinned with
a little cream

Cut the celery into 5 cm/2 inch lengths. Bring a large saucepan of water to the boil. Add the celery and onion, bring back to the boil and cook for 2 minutes. Add the cauliflower, bring back to the boil again and cook for a further 2 minutes.

Meanwhile, cut the French beans into 5 cm/2 inch lengths. Add the beans to the other vegetables. Bring back to the boil, cook for 2 minutes, then drain the vegetables and cool until just warm. Arrange the lettuce in a salad bowl and top with the boiled vegetables. Pour the mayonnaise over and serve at once.

SERVES SIX TO EIGHT

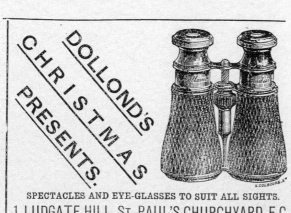
Nesselrode Pudding

24 chestnuts
250 ml/8 fl oz milk
4 egg yolks
150 g/5 oz caster sugar
250 ml/8 fl oz double cream
vanilla essence
50 g/2 oz glacé cherries

Turn the freezing compartment or freezer to the coldest setting about 1 hour before making the pudding.

Using a sharp knife, make a small slit in the rounded side of the shell of each chestnut. Bring a saucepan of water to the boil, add the chestnuts and boil for 5 minutes. Drain. Shell the chestnuts while still very hot. Return them to the clean pan and add 125 ml/4 fl oz of the milk. Simmer gently until the chestnuts are tender, then rub them through a fine sieve into a bowl. Put the egg yolks in a bowl and beat lightly. Pour the milk on to the egg yolks, stirring well. Return the mixture to the clean pan and simmer, stirring constantly, until the custard thickens. Do not let it boil. Remove the custard from the heat and stir in the chestnut purée and the sugar. Leave until cool.

In a bowl, whip half the cream to soft peaks. Add to the chestnut mixture with a few drops of vanilla essence. Pour into a suitable bowl for freezing, cover and freeze until half-frozen (when ice crystals appear around the edge of the mixture).

Meanwhile rinse the cherries, pat dry on absorbent kitchen paper, and chop finely. In a bowl, whip the remaining cream until stiff.

Beat the ice cream mixture until smooth, scraping off the crystals. Stir in the chopped cherries and fold in the whipped cream. Return to the freezer until almost set, stirring the mixture frequently. Press into a 750 ml/1¼ pint mould, cover, and return to the freezer until firm. Return the freezer to the normal setting. Transfer the pudding to the refrigerator about 15 minutes before serving, to allow it to soften and 'ripen'.

SERVES SIX

Meringues

Keep a batch of meringues in an airtight tin at Christmas time and you'll never be short of the means to make an instant dessert or teatime treat.

4 egg whites
pinch of salt
200 g/7 oz caster sugar, plus extra for dusting
1.25 ml/¼ tsp baking powder (optional)

Line a baking sheet with oiled greaseproof paper or with non-stick baking parchment. Set the oven at 110°C/225°F/gas ¼.

Make the meringue mixture as described in the recipe for Mini Meringues on page 139. Put the mixture into a piping bag fitted with a large nozzle and pipe into rounds on the baking parchment. Alternatively, shape the mixture using two wet tablespoons: take up a spoonful of the mixture and smooth it with a palette knife, bringing it up into a ridge in the centre. Slide it out with the other spoon on to the prepared baking sheet, with the ridge on top.

Dust the meringues lightly with caster sugar, then dry off in the oven for 3-4 hours, until they are firm and crisp but still white. If the meringues begin to brown, prop the oven door open a little. When they are crisp on the outside, lift the meringues carefully off the sheet, using a palette knife. Turn them on to their sides and return to the oven until the bases are dry. Cool on a wire rack.

MAKES 24 TO 30 MEDIUM MERINGUES

Rich Chocolate Sauce

Poured over ice cream, on profiteroles, with steamed pudding or, very simply, with canned pears, Rich Chocolate Sauce makes an invaluable standby in the festive season.

350 g/12 oz bitter-sweet chocolate,
roughly grated
45 ml/3 tbsp butter
30 ml/2 tbsp butter
30 ml/2 tbsp double cream
5 ml/1 tsp whisky

Put the grated chocolate in a saucepan with 200 ml/7 fl oz water. Heat gently, stirring all the time, until the chocolate melts. Do not let the sauce boil. Add the butter, 5 ml/1 tsp at a time, and continue stirring until it melts.

Remove the sauce from the heat and stir in the cream and whisky. Serve at once.

MAKES ABOUT 500 ML/17 FL OZ

FREEZER TIP

The sauce may be poured into a heatproof container with a lid, cooled quickly and then frozen for up to 3 months. To use, thaw for 4 hours at room temperature, then stand the container in a saucepan of very hot water until warm.

Informal Dinner Party

> **MENU**
> *Mock Turtle Soup*
>
> *Carbonnade of Beef*
> *Stir-fried Red Cabbage*
> *Broccoli with Toasted Almonds*
> *Boiled Potatoes with*
> *Parsley Butter*
>
> *Mrs Beeton's Apple Flan*
> *Clotted or Whipped Cream*

'The half hour before dinner has always been considered as the great ordeal through which the mistress, in giving a dinner-party, will either pass with flying colours, or lose many of her laurels. The anxiety to receive her guests, - her hope that all will be present in due time, - her trust in the skill of her cook, and the attention of the other domestics, all tend to make these few minutes a trying time.'

Mock Turtle Soup

Traditionally, this Mock Turtle soup was made from a calf's head. This recipe uses stewing veal instead and best results are obtained by using meat on the bone.

25 g/1 oz butter
100 g/4 oz gammon, diced
450 g/1 lb stewing veal, on the bone or in one piece
2 parsley sprigs
2 lemon thyme sprigs
2 marjoram sprigs · 2 basil sprigs
1 large onion, chopped
1 carrot, diced
100 g/4 oz mushrooms, sliced
salt and pepper
30 ml/2 tbsp plain flour
1.75 litres/3 pints good beef stock
150 ml/¼ pint sherry or madeira
juice of 1 lemon
juice of 1 Seville (bitter) orange (optional)
1.25 ml/¼ tsp ground mace
cayenne pepper
about 5 ml/1 tsp sugar
double quantity Mrs Beeton's Forcemeat Balls (page 82)

Melt the butter in a large saucepan. Add the gammon, veal, parsley, lemon thyme, marjoram, basil, onion, carrot, mushrooms and seasoning. Cook, stirring and turning the meat, for 15 minutes. Then stir the flour into the juices surrounding the meat and pour in the stock. Bring to the boil, then lower the heat and cover the pan. Simmer for 2 hours.

Carefully remove the meat from the soup. Discard any bones, dice the meat, and set it aside. Pur_e the remaining contents of the pan in a blender or food processor, or rub through a sieve. Return the soup to a clean pan and add the sherry or madeira, lemon and orange juice, mace, cayenne and sugar to taste. Replace the diced meat and add the fried forcemeat balls. Simmer the soup for 5 minutes to thoroughly reheat the forcemeat balls, then taste for seasoning before serving.

SERVES SIX TO EIGHT

CARBONNADE OF BEEF

Brown ale and long, slow cooking combine to make this classic, full-flavoured stew with its crunchy topping of mustard-seasoned French bread.

50 g/2 oz butter or margarine
675 g/1½ lb stewing steak, trimmed and cut into
4 cm/1½ inch cubes
2 large onions, sliced
1 garlic clove, crushed
15 ml/1 tbsp plain flour
250 ml/8 fl oz beef stock
375 ml/13 fl oz brown ale
salt and pepper ·1 bouquet garni
pinch of grated nutmeg
pinch of soft light brown sugar
5 ml/1 tsp red wine vinegar
6 thin slices of French bread
15 ml/1 tbsp French mustard

Set the oven at 160°C/325°F/gas 3. Melt the butter or margarine in a heavy-bottomed frying pan, add the beef and fry quickly until browned on all sides. Using a slotted spoon, transfer the beef to a casserole and keep hot. Add the onions to the fat remaining in the pan and fry until lightly browned, then stir in the garlic and fry over gentle heat for 1 minute.

Pour off any excess fat from the pan to leave about 15 ml/1 tbsp. Add the flour to the onions and garlic and cook, stirring constantly, until lightly browned. Gradually stir in the stock and ale, with salt and pepper to taste. Add the bouquet garni, nutmeg, brown sugar and vinegar. Bring to the boil, then pour the liquid over the beef. Cover and bake for 1½-2 hours or until tender. Remove the bouquet garni.

Spread the French bread slices with mustard. Arrange them, mustard side up, on top of the carbonnade, pressing them down so that they absorb the gravy. Return the casserole to the oven, uncovered, for about 15 minutes or until the bread browns slightly. Alternatively, place under a hot grill for a few minutes. Serve.

SERVES SIX

MRS BEETON'S APPLE FLAN

6 eating apples
4 cloves
45 ml/3 tbsp medium-dry sherry
30 ml/2 tbsp soft light brown sugar
3 egg whites
45 ml/3 tbsp caster sugar

SHORT CRUST PASTRY
175 g/6 oz plain flour
2.5 ml/½ tsp salt
75 g/3 oz margarine (or half butter, half lard)

Peel and core the apples, cutting each into 8 sections. Place in a heatproof bowl, add the cloves and sherry and cover closely. Place the bowl in a deep saucepan. Add boiling water to come halfway up the sides of the bowl and cook for 20 minutes until the apple sections are tender but still intact.

Set the oven at 200°C/400°F/gas 6. Sift the flour and salt into a bowl, then rub in the margarine. Add enough cold water to make a stiff dough. Roll out the pastry on a lightly floured surface and use to line a 23 cm/9 inch flan tin. Line the pastry with greaseproof paper and fill with baking beans. Bake for 10 minutes. Remove the paper and beans; cook for 5 minutes. Set aside.

Turn the oven temperature down to 140°C/275°F/gas 1. Arrange the apples in the flan. Sprinkle with 30 ml/2 tbsp of the cooking liquid and the brown sugar.

In a clean, grease-free bowl, whisk the egg whites until stiff. Whisk in 10 ml/2 tsp of the caster sugar and spread lightly over the apples. Sprinkle the remaining sugar over. Bake for 1 hour. Serve the flan warm or cold.

SERVES SIX

A Special Dinner Party

> **MENU**
> *Game Soup*
> *Dinner Rolls*
>
> *Plaice and Oyster Pie*
> *Duchesse Potatoes*
> *Glazed Carrots*
> *Buttered French Beans*
>
> *Liqueur Jelly*
> *Brandy Snaps*

Game Soup

meaty remains of 1 roast pheasant or 2-3 smaller
game birds
25 g/1 oz butter or margarine
50 g/2 oz lean rindless bacon, cubed
1.1 litres/2 pints game stock or well-flavoured beef stock
1 onion, sliced
1 large carrot, sliced
1 bouquet garni · 1 blade of mace
1 chicken liver or 50 g/2 oz calf's liver, trimmed
25 g/1 oz plain flour
15-30 ml/1-2 tbsp port or sherry (optional)
salt and pepper

Cut any large pieces of meat from the carcass(es) of
the game birds. Melt the butter or margarine in a
large frying pan, add the game pieces and bacon
cubes and fry over moderate heat for 4-5 minutes.
Set the pan aside.

Combine the stock and game bones in a large
heavy-bottomed saucepan. Add the vegetables, bouquet garni and mace. Bring to the boil, lower the
heat, cover and simmer for 2-2½ hours.

Add the liver to the soup pan and simmer for
15 minutes more. Strain the soup through a sieve or
colander into a clean saucepan. Retain the liver in
the sieve but discard the bones. In a blender or food
processor, purée the liver with the fried game pieces
and bacon, adding a little of the fat from the pan.
Transfer the mixture to a small bowl.

Reheat the fat remaining in the frying pan,
add the flour and cook for 4-5 minutes, stirring constantly until nut brown. Gradually stir the mixture
into the meat purée.

Bring the soup to the boil. Remove the pan
from the heat. Stir in the thickened meat purée,
adding about 5 ml/1 tsp at a time. Return the soup to
a gentle heat. Cook, stirring, until the soup thickens
to the desired consistency. Stir in the port or sherry
and add salt and pepper to taste.
Serve with croûtons.

SERVES FOUR

Duchesse Potatoes

450 g/1 lb old potatoes
salt and pepper
25 g/1 oz butter or margarine
1 egg or 2 egg yolks, plus egg for brushing
grated nutmeg (optional)

Grease a baking sheet. Cut the potatoes into pieces
and cook in a saucepan of salted water for 15-20 minutes. Drain thoroughly, then press the potatoes
through a sieve into a large mixing bowl.

Set the oven at 200°C/400°F/gas 6. Beat the
butter or margarine and egg or egg yolks into the
potatoes. Add salt and pepper to taste and the nutmeg, if used. Spoon the mixture into a piping bag fitted with a large rose nozzle. Pipe rounds of potato on
to the prepared baking sheet. Brush with a little
beaten egg. Bake for about 15 minutes, until golden.

SERVES FOUR TO SIX

Plaice and Oyster Pie

12 oysters
6 plaice fillets, skinned
salt and pepper
75 g/3 oz fresh white breadcrumbs
30 ml/2 tbsp chopped parsley
freshly grated nutmeg
75 g/3 oz butter, melted, plus extra for greasing

Set the oven at 190°C/375°F/gas 5. Butter an oven-proof dish. Open the oysters, reserving the liquor. Use a fairly blunt, short, strong knife. Hold an oyster with the curved shell down. Insert the point of the knife into the hinged end of the shell. Prise it open, taking care that the knife does not slip.

Check that the plaice fillets are free of bones, then lay half of them in the dish. Top with half the oysters and sprinkle with salt and pepper. Sprinkle about a third of the breadcrumbs, half the parsley and a little nutmeg over the top. Add a second layer of plaice and oysters.

Pour the reserved oyster liquor over the fish, then trickle half the butter over before adding the remaining breadcrumbs, parsley and a little nutmeg. Trickle the remaining butter over the top. Bake for 40-45 minutes, until golden and cooked.

SERVES FOUR TO SIX

Glazed Carrots

50 g/2 oz butter
575 g/1¼ lb young carrots, scraped but left whole
3 sugar cubes, crushed
1.25 ml/¼ tsp salt · beef stock (see method)
15 ml/1 tbsp chopped parsley to garnish

Melt the butter in a saucepan. Add the carrots, sugar and salt. Pour in enough stock to half cover the carrots. Cook over gentle heat, without covering the pan, for 15-20 minutes or until the carrots are tender.

Shake the pan occasionally to prevent sticking.

Using a slotted spoon, transfer the carrots to a bowl and keep hot. Boil the stock rapidly in the pan until it is reduced to a rich glaze. Return the carrots to the pan, two or three at a time, turning them in the glaze until thoroughly coated. Place on a heated serving dish, garnish with parsley and serve at once.

SERVES SIX

Liqueur Jelly

The amount of sugar required depends on the flavouring used - if you are adding a sweet liqueur, use the smaller quantity; for brandy or other unsweetened spirits such as rum, use the larger amount.

350-450 g/12-16 oz sugar
40 g/1½ oz gelatine
juice of 2 lemons
200 ml/7 fl oz liqueur or spirits, such as brandy, curaçao or maraschino

Place the sugar in a saucepan with 600 ml/1 pint water. heat until the sugar dissolves, then bring the syrup to the boil. Set aside to cool. Sprinkle the gelatine over 300 ml/½ pint water in a heatproof bowl. Leave to stand for 15 minutes, until spongy, then place the bowl over a saucepan of hot water and stir until the gelatine has dissolved completely. Remove from the heat and add the gelatine to the syrup.

Strain the lemon juice into the syrup and stir in the liqueur or spirits. Rinse a 1.4 litre/ 2½ pint mould with cold water, then pour in the jelly and chill until set. To unmould the jelly, rinse a flat platter with cold water, invert the jelly on it and slide it into position before removing the mould.

SERVES SIX

A Vegetarian Dinner Party

MENU
Mrs Beeton's Cheese Puddings
Melon Boats

Tofu Parcels with Watercress
Cream
Red Cabbage with Apples
Leeks in Cheese Sauce
Sauté Potatoes

Bûche de Noël
or
Bombe Diplomate

Mrs Beeton's Cheese Puddings

Use vegetarian cheeses if preferred.

75 g/3 oz butter, melted
50 g/2 oz fresh breadcrumbs
60 ml/4 tbsp milk
4 eggs, separated
salt and pepper
100 g/4 oz Cheshire cheese, finely grated
100 g/4 oz Parmesan cheese, grated

Set the oven at 190°C/375°F/gas 5. Grease 4 individual soufflé dishes or an ovenproof dish with some of the butter. Place the bread in a bowl and sprinkle the milk over. Leave for 5 minutes, then beat in the egg yolks, salt and pepper and both types of cheese.

Whisk the egg whites until stiff. Stir the remaining melted butter into the cheese mixture, then fold in the egg whites. Turn into the dishes and bake for about 30 minutes for individual puddings or 40-45 minutes for a large pudding. Serve at once.

SERVES FOUR

Melon Boats

1 medium ripe melon, cut into 4-6 segments
1 lemon or lime, sliced
sherry or ginger wine (optional)

Using a sharp knife, slice between the melon skin and flesh on each segment to free the flesh but do not remove it. Cut the flesh across into bite-size sections. Gently ease the first row of chunks forward, then move the next row back. Continue moving neighbouring rows in this fashion so that all the pieces are staggered attractively. Three rows are the typical number in melon wedges.

Cut into the centre of each lemon or lime slice, then twist each slice and use a cocktail stick to secure the twists in the melon boats. Sprinkle each portion with sherry or ginger wine, if liked. Serve lightly chilled.

SERVES FOUR TO SIX

Tofu Parcels

fat for greasing
1 carrot, diced
100 g/4 oz fine French beans, thinly sliced
salt and pepper
2 spring onions, chopped
30 ml/2 tbsp chopped parsley
4 large sheets of filo pastry
50 g/2 oz butter, melted or 60 ml/4 tbsp olive oil
100 g/4 oz low-fat soft cheese with garlic and herbs
275 g/10 oz smoked tofu, quartered

WATERCRESS CREAM

1 bunch of watercress, trimmed and chopped
5 ml/1 tsp grated lemon rind
150 ml/¼ pint soured cream, fromage frais or
Greek-style yogurt

Blanch the carrot and French beans in a saucepan of boiling salted water for 2 minutes, then drain and mix with the spring onions and parsley. Set the oven at 200°C/400°F/gas 6. Grease a baking sheet.

Work on 1 sheet of filo at a time, keeping the others covered. Brush the pastry with butter or olive oil and fold it in half. Place a quarter of the soft cheese in the middle, spreading it slightly but taking care not to tear the pastry. Divide the vegetable mixture into quarters. Use a teaspoon to sprinkle half of one portion over the cheese.

Top with a quarter of the tofu, diced, then sprinkle the remainder of the vegetable portion over.

Fold one side of the filo over the filling, brush lightly with butter or oil, then fold the opposite side over, pressing the pastry together. Brush with more fat and fold the two remaining sides over as before to make a neat parcel. Brush the top with a little oil or butter, then invert the parcel on the prepared baking sheet, so that the thicker layers of pastry are underneath. Brush the top with more fat. Repeat with the remaining pastry and filling.

Bake the parcels for about 30 minutes, until golden and crisp. Meanwhile mix the watercress, lemon rind and soured cream, fromage frais or yogurt in a bowl. Add a little salt and pepper. Use a metal slice to transfer the parcels to serving plates and serve at once, with the watercress cream.

SERVES FOUR

MRS BEETON'S TIP

Instead of making individual parcels, use the same filling ingredients to make a pie. Increase the number of filo pastry sheets to line a flan dish, overlapping them and ensuring the pastry is at least two layers thick. Dice the tofu and spread it out with the rest of the filling. Top with more filo, then fold over the excess from lining the dish. Bake at 180°C/350°F/gas 4 for about 45 minutes, to allow the filo base to cook through.

Red Cabbage with Apples

45 ml/3 tbsp oil
1 onion, finely chopped
1 garlic clove, crushed
900 g/2 lb red cabbage, finely shredded
2 large cooking apples
15 ml/1 tbsp soft light brown sugar or golden syrup
juice of ½ lemon
30 ml/2 tbsp red wine vinegar
salt and pepper
15 ml/1 tbsp caraway seeds (optional)

Heat the oil in a large saucepan, add the onion and garlic and fry gently for 5 minutes. Add the cabbage. Peel, core and slice the apples and add them to the pan with the sugar or syrup. Cook over very gentle heat for 10 minutes, shaking the pan frequently.

Add the lemon juice and vinegar, with salt and pepper to taste. Stir in the caraway seeds, if used. Cover and simmer gently for 1-1½ hours, stirring occasionally and adding a little water if the mixture appears dry. Check the seasoning before serving.

SERVES FOUR TO SIX

Buche de Noel

A traditional French Yule Log to be served at Christmas time. The light sponge mixture is flavoured with rum, and chestnut buttercream is used for the filling and decoration.

SPONGE
butter for greasing
100 g/4 oz icing sugar
3 eggs
20 ml/4 tsp rum
65 g/2½ oz self-raising flour
icing sugar for dusting
marrons glacés to decorate

FILLING
2 (440 g/15½ oz) cans unsweetened chestnut purée
275 g/10 oz butter, softened
100 g/4 oz caster sugar
30 ml/2 tbsp rum

Line and grease a 33 x 25 cm/13 x 10 inch Swiss roll tin. Set the oven at 220°C/425°F/gas 7.

Warm a mixing bowl with hot water, then dry it. Sift in the icing sugar, and break in the eggs. Whisk vigorously for 5-10 minutes until the mixture is very light and fluffy. Add the rum while beating. When the mixture resembles meringue, fold in the flour gently. Pour the mixture into the prepared tin and bake for 7 minutes. Meanwhile, prepare a sheet of greaseproof paper 40 x 30 cm/16 x 12 inches in size and dust it with icing sugar.

Remove the sponge from the oven, loosen the sides from the tin if necessary, and turn it on to the greaseproof paper. Peel off the lining paper. Trim the edges of the sponge if crisp. Starting with one of the long sides, roll it up tightly with the greaseproof paper inside. Cool completely.

Meanwhile, prepare the chestnut buttercream for the filling. Turn the purée into a bowl, beat in the softened butter, then add the sugar and rum.

When the sponge is cold, unroll it carefully and remove the paper. Minor blemishes and cracks do not matter since they will be covered with buttercream. Cover the surface of the sponge with just over half the buttercream, laying it on thickly at the further edge. Roll the sponge up again, then place it on a cake board, with the join underneath.

Cover the roll with the remaining buttercream, either using a knife or an icing bag fitted with a ribbon nozzle, imitating the knots and grain of wood. Chill before serving surrounded by marrons glacés.

SERVES SIX TO EIGHT

UNCLE ACK'S CHRISTMAS PARTY.

BOMBE DIPLOMATE

ILLUSTRATED OPPOSITE

The success of this bombe depends largely on the quality of the vanilla ice cream. Use the best available, or make your own.

600 ml/1 pint vanilla ice cream

FILLING
50 g/2 oz crystallized fruit, chopped
30 ml/2 tbsp maraschino liqueur
125 ml/4 fl oz double cream
25 g/1 oz icing sugar, sifted
2 egg whites

Turn the freezing compartment or freezer to the coldest setting about 1 hour before making the bombe. Chill two bowls; a 1.4 litre/2½ pint pudding basin or bombe mould, and a smaller 600 ml/1 pint bowl.

Soften the vanilla ice cream; beat it until smooth. Spoon a layer of the vanilla ice cream into the chilled mould. Centre the smaller bowl inside the mould, with its rim on a level with the top of the mould. Fill the space between the outer mould and the inner bowl with vanilla ice cream. Cover and freeze until firm.

Meanwhile prepare the filling. Put the chopped crystallized fruit into a shallow dish. Pour the liqueur over and set aside for 30 minutes to macerate.

In a bowl, whip the cream with half the sugar. Put the egg whites in a second, grease-free bowl and whisk until stiff. Fold in the remaining sugar. Carefully mix the cream and egg whites together, and add the crystallized fruit, with the liqueur used for soaking. Chill lightly.

When the vanilla ice cream is firm, remove the bowl from the centre of the mould (filling it with warm water if necessary to dislodge it). Fill the centre of the ice cream mould with the maraschino and fruit mixture, covering it with any remaining ice cream.

Put the lid on the bombe mould or cover the basin with foil. Freeze until firm. Return the freezer to the normal setting. To turn out, dip the mould or basin in cold water, and invert on to a chilled serving dish. Transfer to the refrigerator 15 minutes before serving to allow the ice cream to soften and 'ripen'.

SERVES SIX TO EIGHT

FROSTED LEAVES

The following is a first edition recipe for frosting holly leaves: there is an easier way, which is to brush the leaves with a little egg white, then dust them with caster sugar and leave to dry. Holly leaves look particularly good if they are only partially frosted, around the edges.

'TO FROST HOLLY-LEAVES,
for garnishing and decorating
Dessert and Supper Dishes.

Ingredients. - Sprigs of holly, oiled butter, coarsely-powdered sugar.
Mode. - Procure some nice sprigs of holly; pick the leaves from the stalks, and wipe them with a clean cloth free from all moisture; then place them on a dish near the fire, to get thoroughly dry, but not too near to shrivel the leaves; dip them into oiled butter, sprinkle over them some coarsely-powdered sugar, and dry them before the fire. They should be kept in a dry place, as the least damp would spoil their appearance.
Time. - About 10 minutes to dry before the fire.
Seasonable. - These may be made at any time; but are more suitable for winter garnishes, when fresh flowers are not easily obtained.'

MRS BEETON (1861)

Impressive Bombe Diplomate
is the perfect dinner party dessert

FOOD FOR A CROWD

Impromptu gatherings and informal meals shared both with friends and family are great traditions of the festive season. Sail through the task of cooking for a houseful of guests by using practical recipes which are easily cooked in large quantities. Soups are ideal and they may be frozen in advance. Pâtés and potted foods keep well in the refrigerator for 2-3 days as does a batch of home-made mayonnaise which is perfect for dressing plain boiled eggs or favourite salads.

MRS BEETON'S MULLIGATAWNY

25 g/1 oz butter
30 ml/2 tbsp oil
1 chicken, skinned and jointed or 900 g/2 lb chicken portions
4 rindless back bacon rashers, chopped
3 onions, sliced
1 garlic clove, crushed
15 ml/1 tbsp mild curry powder
25 g/1 oz ground almonds
2 litres/3½ pints chicken stock
175 g/6 oz red lentils
salt and pepper
hot boiled rice to serve

Heat the butter and oil in a large, heavy-bottomed saucepan. Add the chicken and brown the joints all over, then remove them from the pan and set aside. Add the bacon, onions and garlic to the fat remaining in the pan and cook over gentle heat for 5 minutes, then stir in the curry powder and cook for 2 minutes more.

In a small bowl, mix the ground almonds to a paste with a little of the stock. Set aside. Add the remaining stock to the pan and return the chicken joints. Bring to the boil, lower the heat and simmer for 1 hour or until the chicken is tender.

Remove the chicken and cut the meat off the bones, then set aside. Skim any fat off the soup. Add the lentils and bring back to the boil. Reduce the heat, cover and simmer the soup for 30 minutes.

Stir the almond paste into the pan and replace the chicken meat. Simmer for a further 5-10 minutes. Taste for seasoning before serving very hot, with boiled rice.

SERVES EIGHT

LEEK AND OAT BROTH

1 litre/1¾ pints chicken stock
3 leeks, trimmed, sliced and washed
1 bay leaf
salt and pepper
60 ml/4 tbsp fine or medium oatmeal
150 ml/¼ pint single cream

Bring the stock and leeks to the boil in a large saucepan. Add the bay leaf and salt and pepper to taste. Lower the heat and simmer for 20 minutes.

Sprinkle the oatmeal into the simmering soup, whisking all the time. Simmer for 5 minutes more. Then cover and simmer gently for a further 15-20 minutes, until thickened. Stir in the cream, reheat without boiling and serve at once.

SERVES FOUR

MRS BEETON'S TIP
Quick-cook porridge oats may be substituted for oatmeal and the soup simmered for just 5 minutes before adding the cream.

POTTED MUSHROOMS

ILLUSTRATED ON PAGE 39

450 g/1 lb mushrooms, finely chopped
50 g/2 oz butter
salt and pepper
pinch of ground allspice
2 anchovy fillets, mashed finely
melted clarified butter (see Mrs Beeton's Tip)

Place the mushrooms in a heavy bottomed saucepan over gentle heat until the juice runs freely. Raise the heat and cook, uncovered, stirring often until all the juice evaporates and the mushrooms are dry.

Add the butter with salt and pepper to taste. Sprinkle with the allspice and continue cooking for about 5 minutes, or until all the butter is absorbed.

Stir in the anchovies and cook for 2 minutes more. Remove from the heat, turn into small pots and leave to cool. Cover with clarified butter. Refrigerate until the butter is firm, then add a second layer of clarified butter. Use within 5 days.

MAKES ABOUT 300 G/11 OZ

MRS BEETON'S TIP

To clarify butter, heat gently until melted, then stand for 2-3 minutes. Carefully pour the clear yellow liquid on top into a clean bowl, leaving the residue behind. This is the clarified butter.

PATE MAISON

ILLUSTRATED ON PAGE 39

8-10 rindless back bacon rashers
100 g/4 oz pig's liver, trimmed and coarsely chopped
100 g/4 oz rindless boned belly of pork, coarsely chopped
225 g/8 oz sausagemeat
225 g/8 oz cold cooked rabbit, finely chopped
1 onion, finely chopped
25 g/1 oz fresh white breadcrumbs
1 egg, beaten
15 ml/1 tbsp milk
75 ml/3 fl oz brandy
salt and pepper
3 bay leaves, to garnish

Set the oven at 180°C/350°F/gas 4. Arrange the bay leaves on the base of a 1.25 litre/2¼ pint rectangular ovenproof dish or terrine. Lay the bacon rashers flat on a board, one at a time, and stretch them with the back of a knife until quite thin. Set aside two or three rashers for the topping and use the rest to line the dish, overlapping them neatly.

Combine the chopped liver, pork, sausagemeat, rabbit, onion and breadcrumbs in a mixing bowl. Stir in the egg, milk and brandy, with salt and pepper to taste. Spoon the mixture into the lined dish, cover with the reserved bacon rashers and then with a lid or foil. Stand the dish in a roasting tin and add enough hot water to come to within 2.5 cm/1 inch of the rim of the tin.

When cooked, weight the pâté and leave to cool. Chill for 18-24 hours. To serve, remove the top bacon rashers and invert the pâté on a platter.

MAKES ABOUT 1 KG/2¼ LB

Potted Venison

100-150 g/4-5 oz butter
1 kg/2¼ lb cooked venison, finely minced
60 ml/4 tbsp port or brown stock
1.25 ml/¼ tsp grated nutmeg
1.25 ml/¼ tsp ground allspice
salt
2.5 ml/½ tsp freshly ground black pepper
melted clarified butter (see Mrs Beeton's Tip, page 65)

Melt 100 g/4 oz of the butter in a saucepan. Add the minced venison, port or stock, spices, salt and pepper. If the meat is very dry, add the remaining butter.

Cook the mixture gently until blended and thoroughly hot. Immediately turn into small pots and leave to cool. Cover with clarified butter. When cool, refrigerate until the butter is firm.

MAKES ABOUT 1 KG/2¼ LB

Potted Shrimps or Prawns

225 g/8 oz unsalted butter
450 g/1 lb peeled cooked shrimps or prawns
1.25 ml/¼ tsp ground white pepper
1.25 ml/¼ tsp ground mace
1.25 ml/¼ tsp ground cloves
dill sprigs to garnish

Melt the butter in a saucepan, add the shrimps or prawns and heat very gently, without boiling. Add the pepper, mace and cloves.

Using a slotted spoon, transfer the shrimps or prawns to small pots. Pour a little of the hot spiced butter into each pot.

Set the remaining spiced butter aside until the residue has settled, then pour over the shrimps or prawns. Chill until the butter is firm. Store in a refrigerator for up to 48 hours. Garnish with dill.

MAKES ABOUT 675 G/1½ LB

Mayonnaise

Buy eggs from a reputable supplier and make sure they are perfectly fresh. Immediately before using wash the eggs in cold water and dry them on absorbent kitchen paper.

2 egg yolks · salt and pepper
5 ml/1 tsp caster sugar
5 ml/1 tsp Dijon mustard
about 30 ml/2 tbsp lemon juice
250 ml/8 fl oz oil (olive oil or a mixture of olive and grapeseed or sunflower oil)

Place the egg yolks in a medium or large bowl. Add salt and pepper, the sugar, mustard and 15 ml/1 tbsp of the lemon juice. Whisk thoroughly until the sugar has dissolved. An electric whisk is best.

Whisking all the time, add the oil drop by drop so that it forms an emulsion with the egg yolks. As the oil is incorporated, and the mixture begins to turn pale, it may be added in a slow trickle. If the oil is added too quickly before it begins to combine with the eggs, the sauce will curdle.

When all the oil has been incorporated the mayonnaise should be thick and pale. Taste the mixture, then stir in more lemon juice, salt and pepper, if necessary. Keep mayonnaise in a covered container in the refrigerator for up to 5 days.

MAKES ABOUT 300 ML/½ PINT

Coleslaw

450 g/1 lb firm white or Savoy cabbage, finely shredded
100 g/4 oz carrots, coarsely grated
2 celery sticks, thinly sliced
½ small green pepper, seeded and thinly sliced
150 ml/¼ pint mayonnaise or plain yogurt
salt and pepper · lemon juice (see method)

Mix all the ingredients in a salad bowl, adding enough lemon juice to give the mayonnaise or yogurt a tangy taste. Chill before serving.

SERVES FOUR

MRS BEETON'S POTATO SALAD

10 small cold cooked potatoes
60 ml/4 tbsp tarragon vinegar
90 ml/6 tbsp salad oil · salt and pepper
15 ml/1 tbsp chopped parsley

Cut the potatoes into 1 cm/½ inch thick slices. For the dressing, mix the tarragon vinegar, oil and plenty of salt and pepper in a screw-topped jar. Close the jar tightly and shake vigorously until well blended.

Layer the potatoes in a salad bowl, sprinkling with a little dressing and the parsley. Pour over any remaining dressing, cover and set aside to marinate before serving.

SERVES SIX

VARIATIONS

Potato and Anchovy Salad Drain a 50 g/2 oz can of anchovy fillets, reserving the oil. Chop the fillets. Use the oil to make the dressing. Sprinkle the chopped anchovies between the layers of potato with the dressing.
Potato and Olive Salad Thinly slice 50 g/2 oz stoned black olives. Chop 2 spring onions, if liked, and mix them with the olives. Sprinkle the olives between the potato layers.

PINEAPPLE AND KIRSCH SALAD

4 small pineapples
225 g/8 oz black grapes
2 bananas
2 pears
15–30 ml/1–2 tbsp lemon juice
45 ml/3 tbsp kirsch
sugar

Cut the pineapples in half lengthways. Cut out the core from each, then scoop out the flesh, using first a knife, then a spoon, but taking care to keep the pineapple shells intact. Discard the core, and working over a bowl, chop the flesh.

Add the pineapple flesh to the bowl. Halve the grapes and remove the pips. Add to the pineapple mixture. Peel and slice the bananas; peel, core, and slice the pears. Put the lemon juice in a shallow bowl, add the pear and banana slices and toss both fruits before adding to the pineapple and grapes. Mix all the fruit together, pour the kirsch over and sweeten to taste with the sugar. Pile the fruit back into the pineapple shells and chill until required.

SERVES EIGHT

MRS BEETON'S TIPSY CAKE

1 (15 cm/6 inch) sponge cake
30 ml/2 tbsp redcurrant jelly
75 ml/3 fl oz brandy
50 g/2 oz whole blanched almonds
375 ml/13 fl oz milk
125 ml/4 fl oz single cream
8 egg yolks
75 g/3 oz caster sugar
extra redcurrant jelly to decorate

Put the cake in a glass bowl or dish 16 cm/6 inches in diameter and slightly deeper than the cake. Spread the cake thinly with jelly, then pour over as much brandy as the cake can absorb. Cut the almonds lengthways into spikes and stick them all over the top of the cake.

Mix the milk and cream in a bowl. In a second, heatproof, bowl beat the yolks until liquid, and pour the milk and cream over them. Stir in the sugar. Transfer the mixture to the top of a double saucepan and cook over gently simmering water for about 20 minutes or until the custard thickens, stirring all the time. Let the custard cool slightly, then pour it over and around the cake. Cover with dampened greaseproof paper. When cold, refrigerate the tipsy cake for about 1 hour. Decorate with small spoonfuls of redcurrant jelly and serve.

SERVES FOUR TO SIX

DANISH APPLE CAKE

The quantities for this simply delicious dessert can easily be increased to cater for a crowd.

1 kg/2¼ lb cooking apples
150 g/5 oz dried white breadcrumbs
75 g/3 oz sugar
100–125 g/4–4½ oz butter

DECORATION
300 ml/½ pint whipping cream
red jam, melted

Set the oven at 180°C/350°F/gas 4. Place the apples on a baking sheet and bake for 1 hour. When cool enough to handle, remove the peel and core from each apple; purée the fruit in a blender or food processor or rub through a sieve into a bowl.

In a separate bowl, mix the breadcrumbs with the sugar. Melt the butter in a frying pan, add the crumb mixture, and fry until golden.

Place alternate layers of crumbs and apple purée in a glass dish, starting and finishing with crumbs.

Whip the cream in a bowl and put into a piping bag fitted with a large star nozzle. Decorate the top of the apple cake with cream rosettes and drizzle a little red jam over the top. Chill before serving.

SERVES FOUR TO SIX

THE CHEESEBOARD

A well–chosen selection of cheeses is invaluable when the house is full of guests and numbers tend to vary from meal to meal. With plenty of good bread in the freezer, a tin stocked with oatcakes and crackers, and a selection of chutneys and pickles in the cupboard, there will always be hearty and quickly prepared refreshments for any number of guests.

STORING AND PRESENTING CHEESE

Cheese should be wrapped and stored in an airtight container in the refrigerator, and brought just to room temperature before serving. Do not leave the cheese out, particularly uncovered, for long periods but replace it in the refrigerator promptly after each meal.

Hard and soft cheeses are usually served separately, with different knives. Blue cheese should be separated from other cheeses, especially when it is soft and ripe. Flavoured cheeses are also best served separately from plain cheese.

Grapes, dates and nuts may be offered with the cheese or arranged on the cheeseboard. Celery sticks, apples and pears are also excellent accompaniments. For lunch or supper, mustard, pickles, chutneys are relishes may be offered as well as black or green olives.

HARD CHEESE

Include a good Cheddar which will go well with pickled onions and crusty bread. A lighter, tangy cheese, such as Wensleydale or Cheshire, is preferred by some. Red Windsor and Sage Derby are two examples of traditional flavoured cheeses, the first flavoured with red wine. Buttery Jarlesberg, well–matured Gouda or Emmental or Gruyère are also useful cheeses which marry well with fruit for the final course of a meal. When there is a good stock of pickles and relishes, it is best to avoid the cheeses which are flavoured with nuts, pickles or garlic as there is a danger of including too many different flavours on a cheeseboard served for lunch or a light meal.

Stilton is the traditional cheese for Christmas and small whole cheeses, half cheeses or slices off a larger cheese are readily available at this time of year.

A whole cheese may be served by scooping or by cutting off wedges radiating from the centre of the cheese. In the first edition, Mrs Beeton describes methods for improving the flavour of under–ripe cheese, particularly that of pouring port into the scooped–out cheese and allowing this to mature before serving; however, these methods are not to be recommended today.

'Stilton cheese, or British Parmesan, as it is sometimes called, is generally preferred to all other cheeses by those whose authority few will dispute.

Cheeses made in May or June are usually served at Christmas; or, to be in prime order, should be kept from 10 – 12 months, or even longer. An artificial ripeness in Stilton cheese is sometimes produced by inserting a small piece of decayed Cheshire into an aperture at the top.

From 3 weeks to a month is sufficient time to ripen the cheese. An additional flavour may also be obtained by scooping out a piece from the top, and pouring therein port, sherry, Madeira, or old ale, and letting the cheese absorb these for 2 or 3 weeks, but that cheese is the finest which is ripened without any artificial aid, is the opinion of those who are judges in these matters. In serving a Stilton cheese, the top of it should be cut off to form a lid, and a napkin or piece of white paper, with a frill at the top, pinned round. When the cheese goes from table, the lid should be replaced.'

MRS BEETON (1861)

POPULAR SOFT CHEESES

Brie and Camembert are versatile favourites which go down well after a meal or can form the basis of a light lunch or supper. Buying a small or large whole Brie is a good idea if you are planning a party. There are many types of Brie, varying greatly in respect of depth of flavour and exact texture, and the quality of the cheese, as well as its ripeness, will depend on the supplier.

STILTON CHEESE.

CHRISTMAS EVE

Christmas Eve Supper

Fish is traditionally eaten on Christmas Eve in many countries. Being light, it is perfect to precede the Christmas feast.

MENU
Crudités with Dips

Baked Fish with Oyster Stuffing
Diced Carrots with Green Beans
Sautéed Mushrooms with Chives
Steamed Potatoes with Parsley Butter

Lemon Water Ice

Instead of a formal first course, offer dips and a selection of crudités with drinks before the meal. Keep the dips simple, for example offer soured cream with snipped chives or soft cheese flavoured with chopped herbs. Mash some Stilton cheese with soft cheese and a little soured cream to make a full-flavoured dip or combine chopped hard-boiled eggs with soft cheese, mayonnaise and snipped chives.

Prepare sticks of carrot and celery, small cauliflower florets and fingers of cucumber for dipping. Breadsticks and small crackers or plain savoury biscuits may also be served with the dips. Avoid highly seasoned bought snacks or crisps as they will spoil the palate before the delicate fish main course.

Baked Fish with Oyster Stuffing

Once a common food, oysters are central to many traditional English dishes. Rich in protein and full of flavour, they make an excellent stuffing for a whole fish such as grey mullet or could be used as a stuffing for steak.

2 (1 kg/2¼ lb) grey mullet, scaled, cleaned and trimmed
2-3 rindless bacon rashers
lemon wedges to garnish

OYSTER STUFFING
12 fresh or canned oysters
225 g/8 oz fresh white breadcrumbs
100 g/4 oz shredded suet or melted butter
10 ml/2 tsp chopped mixed fresh herbs
1.25 ml/¼ tsp grated nutmeg
salt and pepper
2 eggs

Set the oven at 180°C/350°F/gas 4. Make the stuffing. If using fresh oysters, open them over a saucepan (see Plaice and Oyster Pie, page 58), then simmer them very gently in their own liquor for 10 minutes. Canned oysters need no cooking. Drain the oysters, reserving the liquor, and cut into small pieces.

In a bowl, mix the breadcrumbs with the suet or melted butter. Add the oysters, herbs and nutmeg, with salt and pepper to taste. Beat the eggs in a cup until just liquid, then stir enough of the egg into the oyster mixture to moisten. The stuffing must not be sloppy.

Stuff the fish with the oyster mixture. Place them in an ovenproof dish or on a baking sheet. Lay the bacon rashers over the top of each and bake for 25-30 minutes.

Transfer to a warmed platter, garnish with the lemon wedges and serve at once.

SERVES FOUR TO SIX

*Crisp Filo Pastries (page 75)
are tempting accompaniments
for a Christmas Eve drink*

LEMON WATER ICE

Water ices are simple desserts made from fruit or flavoured syrup or a combination of fruit purée and sugar syrup. They are usually beaten halfway through the freezing process, but may be frozen without stirring, in which case they are called granités. When hot syrup is used as the basis for a water ice, it must be allowed to cool before freezing.

6 lemons
2 oranges

SYRUP
350 g/12 oz caster sugar
5 ml/1 tsp liquid glucose

Turn the freezing compartment or freezer to the coldest setting about 1 hour before making the lemon water ice.

Make the syrup. Put the sugar in a heavy-bottomed saucepan with 250 ml/8 fl oz water. Dissolve the sugar over a gentle heat, stirring occasionally. Bring to the boil and boil steadily, without stirring, for about 10 minutes or to a temperature of 110°C/225°F. Remove any scum from the surface.

Strain the syrup into a large bowl and stir in the liquid glucose. Pare the rind very thinly from the lemons and oranges and add to the bowl of syrup. Cover and cool.

Squeeze the fruit and add the juice to the cold syrup mixture. Strain through a nylon sieve into a suitable container for freezing.

Cover the container closely and freeze until half-frozen (when ice crystals appear around the edge of the mixture). Beat the mixture thoroughly, scraping off any crystals. Replace the cover and freeze until solid. Return the freezer to the normal setting.

Transfer the water ice to the refrigerator about 15 minutes before serving, to allow it to soften and 'ripen'. Serve in scoops in individual dishes.

SERVES SIX

Family Supper Dishes

Christmas Eve is often a working day as well as the end of lengthy domestic preparations, so a simple family supper provides the perfect opportunity for relaxing into the holiday spirit.

CAULIFLOWER WITH MUSHROOM SAUCE

1 kg/2¼ lb cauliflower
50 g/2 oz butter
25 g/1 oz plain flour
375 ml/13 fl oz vegetable stock or milk
175 g/6 oz button mushrooms, finely chopped
4 egg yolks
15 ml/1 tbsp lemon juice
salt and pepper
pinch of grated nutmeg
6 slices of bread
butter

Break the cauliflower into medium florets and boil or steam them until just tender. Drain thoroughly and keep hot.

Melt the butter in a saucepan, stir in the flour and cook for 1 minute. Gradually add the stock or milk, stirring constantly until the sauce boils and thickens. Add the mushrooms to the sauce, lower the heat and simmer gently for 5 minutes.

Beat the egg yolks lightly in a small bowl. Beat in the lemon juice and 30 ml/ 2 tbsp of the hot sauce, then stir into the remaining sauce. Heat gently, but do not allow the sauce to boil after the egg yolks have been added or it will curdle. Stir in salt and pepper to taste and add the nutmeg.

Toast the bread, stamp out rounds with a plain cutter, and butter each one. Arrange the cauliflower neatly on the toast and pour the sauce over. Serve.

SERVES SIX

Mrs Beeton's Potato Rissoles

These rissoles may be cooked ahead and frozen. Cool the cooked rissoles quickly, open freeze them on baking sheets or trays, then pack into polythene bags or rigid containers. Freeze for up to 3 months.

50 g/2 oz butter
1 large onion, finely chopped
350 g/12 oz hot mashed potato
salt and pepper
10 ml/2 tsp chopped parsley
2 eggs, beaten
75 g/3 oz dried white breadcrumbs
oil for shallow frying

Melt half the butter in a frying pan. Cook the onion, stirring often, until soft but not browned. Season the mashed potato generously, then stir in the parsley and onion with all the butter from the pan. Allow the mixture to cool completely. When cold, shape the mixture into small balls.

Put the beaten egg in a shallow bowl and the breadcrumbs on a plate or sheet of foil. Dip the potato rissoles in the egg, then coat them thoroughly in breadcrumbs. Place them on a baking sheet and chill for 15 minutes to firm the mixture.

Heat the remaining butter with the oil for shallow frying in a deep frying pan. Put in the rissoles and turn them in the hot fat for 6-9 minutes until golden brown all over. Drain on absorbent kitchen paper and serve hot.

MAKES ABOUT TEN

Spanish Omelette

Known as tortilla, a Spanish omelette is quite different from filled and folded omelettes or feather-light soufflé omelettes. It is a thick cake of potato and onion set in egg, cut into wedges and served hot or cold. This classic potato omelette is quite delicious without any additional ingredients; however, the recipe is often varied to include red and green peppers or a mixture of vegetables, such as peas and green beans.

675 g/1½ lb potatoes
225 g/8 oz onions, thinly sliced
salt and pepper
45 ml/3 tbsp olive oil
6 eggs, beaten

Cut the potatoes into 1 cm/½ inch cubes and mix them with the onions in a basin. Add plenty of seasoning and mix well.

Heat the oil in a heavy-bottomed frying pan which has fairly deep sides. Add the potatoes and onions, then cook, stirring and turning the vegetables often, until both potatoes and onions are tender. This takes about 25 minutes.

Pour the eggs over the potatoes and cook over medium heat, stirring, until the eggs begin to set. Press the vegetables down evenly and leave to set. Lower the heat to prevent the base of the omelette overbrowning before the eggs have set sufficiently.

Lay a large plate over the omelette and invert the pan to turn the omelette out on the plate. The base of the pan should be well greased but if it looks a little dry, add a little extra olive oil and heat it. Slide the omelette back into the pan and cook over medium to high heat for 35 minutes, until crisp and browned. Serve the omelette hot, warm or cold.

SERVES FOUR TO SIX

Spaghetti alla Carbonara

450 g/1 lb spaghetti
salt and pepper
15 ml/1 tbsp oil
100 g/4 oz rindless streaky bacon rashers,
cut into fine strips
4 eggs
30 ml/2 tbsp double cream
75 g/3 oz Pecorino or Parmesan cheese, grated

Cook the spaghetti in a large saucepan of boiling salted water for 8-10 minutes or until tender but still firm to the bite.

Meanwhile heat the oil in a large frying pan and fry the bacon until the fat is transparent. Draw the pan off the heat. In a bowl, beat the eggs with the cream, adding a little salt and a generous grinding of pepper.

Drain the cooked spaghetti thoroughly and mix it with the bacon. Return to moderate heat for 1-2 minutes to heat through. Stir the egg mixture rapidly into the pan. As it begins to thicken, tip in the cheese. Do not stir it in. Serve immediately on hot plates.

SERVES FOUR

MRS BEETON'S TIP
Use fresh pasta with this sauce, if preferred. It will cook in considerably less time than dried pasta and will be ready as soon as it rises to the surface of the boiling water. Test after 1 minute.

Finger Food

The festivities may begin on Christmas Eve with friends arriving for a light lunch, an afternoon tipple or early evening drinks. Simple-to-serve, cook-ahead finger food goes down well for lunch or supper - here are a few suggestions.

Mrs Beeton's Scotch Eggs

4 rindless back bacon rashers, finely chopped
50 g/2 oz shredded suet
75 g/3 oz wholemeal breadcrumbs
15 ml/1 tbsp grated lemon rind
5 ml/1 tsp finely chopped parsley
1.25 ml/¼ tsp dried oregano
pinch of ground mace
salt and cayenne pepper
Worcestershire sauce
2 eggs, beaten
75 g/3 oz fresh white breadcrumbs
15 ml/1 tbsp plain flour
salt and pepper
4 hard-boiled eggs
oil for deep frying

Combine the bacon, suet, breadcrumbs, lemon rind, herbs and mace in a bowl. Add salt, cayenne and Worcestershire sauce to taste. Stir in enough of the beaten egg to make a forcemeat which can be shaped.

Beat the remaining beaten egg with 10 ml/2 tsp water in a small bowl. Spread out the breadcrumbs in a second, shallow bowl. Divide the forcemeat into 4 equal pieces. On a lightly floured surface, pat each piece into a circle about 13 cm/5 inches in diameter.

Mix the remaining flour with the salt and pepper in a sturdy polythene bag. Add the hard-boiled eggs and toss gently to coat evenly. Place an egg in the centre of each circle of forcemeat. Mould the forcemeat evenly round the egg, making sure it fits snugly. Seal the joins with a little of the beaten egg

mixture and pinch well together.

Mould each Scotch egg to a good shape, brush all over with beaten egg, then roll in the breadcrumbs until evenly coated. Press the crumbs well in.

Put the oil for frying into a deep saucepan and heat to 160℃/325°F or until a cube of bread added to the oil browns in 2 minutes. If using a deep fat fryer, follow the manufacturer's instructions. Add the eggs carefully and fry for about 10 minutes until golden brown. Lift out with a slotted spoon and drain on absorbent kitchen paper. Serve hot or cold.

SERVES FOUR

Filo Pastries

ILLUSTRATED ON PAGE 71

225 g/8 oz feta cheese
5 ml/1 tsp dried oregano
1 spring onion, chopped
pepper
4 sheets of filo pastry
50 g/2 oz butter, melted

Set the oven at 190℃/375°F/gas 5. Mash the feta with the oregano in a bowl, then mix in the spring onion and pepper to taste.

Lay a sheet of filo pastry on a clean, dry surface and brush it with melted butter. Cut the sheet widthways into 9 strips. Place a little feta mixture at one end of the first strip, leaving the corner of the pastry without filling. Fold the corner over the feta to cover it in a triangular shape, then fold the mixture over and over to wrap it in several layers of pastry, making a small triangular-shaped pasty.

Repeat with the other strips of pastry. Cut and fill the remaining sheets in the same way to make 36 triangular pastries. Place these on baking sheets and brush any remaining butter over them. Bake for about 10 minutes, until crisp and golden. Transfer the triangles to a wire rack to cool. Serve warm.

MAKES 36

SHAPES

The feta filling used in the triangles is a Greek speciality. A variety of other fillings may be used and the pastry shaped in other ways.

Instead of cutting strips, the pastry may be cut into squares (about 6 per sheet). The filling should be placed in the middle of the squares, and the pastry may be gathered up to form a small bundle. The butter coating keeps the bundle closed when the filo is pressed together. For strength, the filo may be used double.

Alternatively, squares of filo may be filled and folded into neat oblong parcels. Oblong pieces of filo (about 4 per sheet) may be folded into neat squares.

FILLINGS

Spinach and Cheese Thoroughly drained cooked spinach may be used with or without the cheese. Flavour plain spinach with chopped spring onion and grated nutmeg.

Sardine Mashed canned sardines in tomato sauce make a good filling for filo triangles.

Chicken or Ham Chopped cooked chicken or ham are both tasty fillings for filo. Combine them with a little low-fat soft cheese.

Apricot Apricot halves (drained canned or fresh) topped with a dot of marmalade make good sweet filo pastries. Dust them with icing sugar after baking.

Apple and Almond Mix some ground almonds into cold, sweetened apple purée. Use to fill triangles or squares.

PASTRY HORNS

225 g/8 oz puff pastry
flour for rolling out
beaten egg and milk for glazing

Roll out the pastry 5 mm/¼ inch thick on a lightly floured surface, then cut into strips 35 cm/14 inches long and 2 cm/¾ inch wide. Moisten the strips with cold water.

Wind each strip around a cornet mould, working from the point upward, keeping the moistened surface on the outside. Lay the horns on a dampened baking sheet, with the final overlap of the pastry strip underneath. Leave in a cool place for 1 hour.

Set the oven at 220°C/425°F/gas 7. Brush the horns with beaten egg and milk. Bake for 10-15 minutes or until golden brown. Remove the moulds and return the horns to the oven for 5 minutes. Cool completely on a wire rack. When cold, fill the horns with a sweet or savoury filling.

MAKES EIGHT

VOL-AU-VENT CASES

400 g/14 oz puff pastry
flour for rolling out
beaten egg for glazing

Set the oven at 220°C/425°F/gas 7. Roll out the pastry on a lightly floured surface about 2 cm/¾ inch thick (1 cm/½ inch thick for bouchées).Cut into round or oval shapes as liked. Place on a baking sheet and brush the top of the pastry with beaten egg.

With a smaller, floured cutter, make a circular or oval cut in each case, to form an inner ring, cutting through about half the depth of the pastry. Bake for 20-25 minutes until golden brown and crisp.

When baked, remove the inner circular or oval lid, then scoop out the soft inside while still warm to make room for the filling.

MAKES TWENTY-FOUR 5 CM/2 INCH OR TWELVE 7.5 CM/
3 INCH BOUCHEES OR EIGHT 9 CM/3 INCH OR TWO 15 CM/
6 INCH VOL-AU-VENT CASES

MRS BEETON'S TIP
For a better appearance a separate piece of pastry can be baked for the lid instead of using the centre portion of the case.

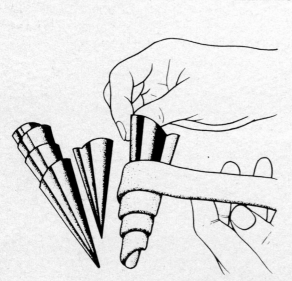

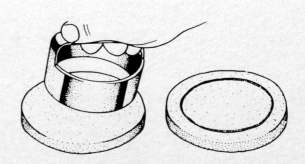

LARGE DEEP VOL-AU-VENT

A large deep vol-au-vent should be made for serving with a hot, savoury sauced filling, a hot dessert filling, such as stewed fruit, or a pile of strawberries topped with whipped cream. The pastry should be prepared as for the previous recipe and the oven preheated. The pastry should be rolled to a thickness of 3.5 cm/1½ inches. Use a plate to stamp out the vol-au-vent. It is possible to buy large cutters, plain and fluted, from specialist cookshops and catering suppliers. Bake as for small vol-au-vent cases, allowing an extra 5 minutes' cooking if necessary.

FILLINGS FOR PASTRY HORNS AND VOL-AU-VENT CASES

The basic pastry cases may be filled in a variety of ways, both savoury and sweet.

Seafood Filling For vol-au-vent cases. Melt 25 g/1 oz butter in a saucepan. Stir in 25 g/1 oz plain flour, then cook for 1 minute. Pour in 300 ml/½ pint milk, stirring all the time, and bring to the boil. Simmer for 3 minutes. Add a 200 g/7 oz can tuna (drained), 100 g/4 oz frozen peeled cooked prawns and seasoning to taste. Stir in 30 ml/2 tbsp chopped parsley and simmer for 3 minutes, stirring occasionally until the prawns are thawed. Spoon into the pastry cases and serve hot.

Hot Chicken Make the sauce as for seafood filling, using half milk and half chicken stock. Instead of adding tuna, add 225 g/8 oz diced cooked chicken meat and 50 g/2 oz sliced button mushrooms. Season with a little nutmeg, then simmer gently for 5 minutes. Stir in 60 ml/4 tbsp single cream and a little chopped tarragon or parsley. Heat gently but do not boil.

Ham and Tomato Mix 50 g/2 oz diced cooked ham with 2 peeled and diced tomatoes, 1 chopped spring onion and 100 g/4 oz soft cheese (full-fat soft cheese, ricotta, quark or low-fat soft cheese). Add salt and pepper to taste, then spoon into the cold pastry cases.

Chicken Mayonnaise Dice 100 g/4 oz cooked chicken and bind with mayonnaise to a creamy mixture. Add 30 ml/2 tbsp snipped chives and salt and pepper to taste, then spoon the mixture into the cold pastry cases.

Spiced Turkey Dice 100-175 g/4-6 oz cooked turkey and mix with 15 ml/1 tbsp mango chutney. Cook 1 chopped onion in 25 g/1 oz butter until soft, stir in 5 ml/1 tsp curry powder and cook for 2 minutes. Stir into the turkey, then bind with mayonnaise.

Stewed Fruit Filling Apples, plums or other fresh fruit may be used to fill a large hot dessert vol-au-vent. Heat 50-75 g/2-3 oz sugar and 300 ml/½ pint water until the sugar dissolves. Bring to the boil. Add the chosen prepared fruit and cook gently, turning occasionally, until tender. Use a slotted spoon to transfer the fruit to a dish. Boil the syrup until well reduced and thickened. Spoon the fruit into the vol-au-vent, then pour the thick syrup over. Dust the filling with icing sugar and serve at once.

Jam and Cream Place 5 ml/1 tsp jam in each pastry case, then top with whipped cream. The cream may be flavoured with a little liqueur (such as Grand Marnier) or sherry and sweetened with a little caster or icing sugar before whipping. Sprinkle chopped nuts over the cream filling, if liked.

Fruit Horns Roughly chopped fresh fruit, such as strawberries or peaches, may be mixed with lightly sweetened whipped cream to fill the pastry cases.

Chocolate Cream Stir 45 ml/3 tbsp boiling water into 15 ml/1 tbsp cocoa. Add 30 ml/2 tbsp brandy or chocolate liqueur. Mix in 300 ml/½ pint double cream and 30 ml/2 tbsp icing sugar. Whip the cream until it stands in soft peaks. Pipe or spoon it into the pastries.

THE HOLLY AND THE IVY

CHRISTMAS DAY

The Christmas Meal

Christmas Day can be one of the very few occasions - if not the only one - when a crowd gathers together for a large, and formal, meal and if you are not used to cooking for so many people this can be a nightmare. The solution is to plan ahead, make the maximum use of the freezer and enlist the help of all the other members of the household. That way the cook joins in the festivities along with the rest of the family and any guests.

MENU
Smoked Salmon

Roast Turkey
Mrs Beeton's Forcemeat
Sage and Onion Stuffing
Roast Potatoes
Brussels Sprouts with Chestnuts
Braised Celery
Glazed Carrots
Bread Sauce or Gravy
Cranberry Sauce

Plum Pudding
Plum Pudding Sauce
or
Brandy Sauce

Ideas for Simple Starters

＊ Smoked salmon served with lemon juice and black pepper. ＊ Avocado with a simple dressing of oil and vinegar. Add a little walnut oil and snipped chives to the dressing. ＊ Sliced ripe pears with crumbled crisply cooked bacon, a little crumbled Stilton cheese and a dressing of oil and lemon juice. ＊ Parma ham with freshly ground black pepper and lime or lemon juice. ＊ Parma ham with thin slices of melon. ＊ A light consommé with thinly sliced mushrooms added.

Selecting the Menu

The menu seldom poses many problems, with the main choice being the roast of the day. Turkey is the most popular; however, a goose may be served instead or you may prefer to cook a glorious joint of beef. A boned breast of turkey is a good option for smaller households or those who prefer not to have large quantities of cold roast to consume. Roast potatoes are easy to prepare and save hob space which can be at a premium if there are several other vegetables and the pudding to cook. It is a good idea to serve at least one, if not two, plain vegetables, such as Brussels sprouts or carrots, and braised vegetables or other mixed vegetable dishes should be selected with care.

The first course must not be too heavy or rich. It should do no more than awaken the taste buds before a traditional main course. A little smoked salmon, avocado, melon or a small portion of light soup would be ideal. Avoid creamy dressings and heavy soups which will leave everyone feeling full. Crisp, very thin melba toast may be made a couple of days ahead and stored in an airtight container for

Roast Turkey (page 82) with Mrs Beeton's Forcemeat (page 82), Chestnut Stuffing (page 82),
Sage and Onion Stuffing (page 83), garnished with Cranberry Sauce (page 85) in satsuma cups;
served with Brussels Sprouts with Chestnuts (page 90), Braised Celery (page 90) and roast potatoes

offering with the first course. You may prefer to miss the first course completely and simply offer a small dish of crisp vegetables with drinks beforehand. Alternatively, cut a few tiny open smoked salmon sandwiches to nibble with aperitifs.

Vegetarian Alternative

Preparing a special and attractive vegetarian menu is not a problem; however, adapting a meal which is primarily based on roast so that it becomes suitable for vegetarians requires a little extra thought. The best approach is to include at least one braised vegetable dish which complements both the vegetarian and roast main dish. This solves the problem of making a separate vegetarian sauce instead of gravy. Prepare a main dish which can be part-cooked ahead and completed with the minimum of fuss, selecting it to complement the vegetables. For example, a dish of semolina gnocchi, finished in the oven, tastes good with braised as well as plain-cooked vegetables and does not need a separate batch of roast potatoes. Alternatively, a loaf based on pulses or a buckwheat bake may be prepared. Again, the important point is that a moist vegetable dish will sauce these vegetarian main courses.

Remember not to use traditional suet in a pudding for vegetarians but opt for vegetable suet instead. A trifle or a mincemeat flan (made with vegetable suet or suet-free mincemeat) are good alternatives to plum pudding.

Planning and Preparing the Meal

* Make the traditional plum pudding well in advance or freeze an alternative pudding a few weeks beforehand. Remember to check the pudding a couple of weeks before Christmas and to 'feed' it with a little brandy.
* Clean out the refrigerator a week or so before Christmas and make sure you have the maximum space available before stocking up with festive food.

* Order the turkey, goose or joint in plenty of time. Check the weight and calculate the thawing time for a frozen bird. Make sure you have refrigerator space or a suitable place for thawing the bird.
* Freeze fresh breadcrumbs up to a couple of months in advance, ready for making stuffings, or make the chosen stuffings a couple of weeks ahead and freeze them. Remember to thaw them on Christmas Eve.
* Make stock for sauces or freeze suitable sauces a couple of weeks ahead.
* Vegetables, such as potatoes and Brussels sprouts, may be prepared on Christmas Eve and stored appropriately: potatoes must be submerged in cold water with a little lemon juice added and kept covered; sprouts and carrots may be stored in a polythene bag in the refrigerator. This is not normally recommended due to the loss of nutrients; however, it is practical for a special occasion meal.
* Prepare apple sauce, cranberry sauce and brandy butter or hard sauce on Christmas Eve.
* Roll bacon rolls on Christmas Eve, cover and chill ready for baking.
* Check and trim the turkey on Christmas Eve, rinsing and drying its body cavity and chilling it ready for stuffing.
* Set the table on Christmas Eve or early on Christmas Day, or delegate this task to one or more members of the family.
* Stuff the turkey shortly before it is due to go into the oven - do not stuff it and leave it for many hours or overnight.
* Prepare the simple first course, if serving, or delegate this task to a competent helper.
* Chill white wine. All red wines except light fruity reds benefit from careful decanting into a carafe or decanter about 1 hour before serving.
* Plan the best use of the hob space: remember that the pudding has to be boiled or steamed for a couple of hours and space must be allowed for vegetables and sauces. If you like, three-quarters cook some of the vegetables and transfer them to suitable covered dishes ready for finishing in the microwave just before serving - this is a good method of preparing

before serving - this is a good method of preparing creamed parsnips, mashed swede or buttered sprouts.

* Have all serving dishes ready and warmed. Transfer the turkey to a warmed serving dish and cover it closely with foil placed shiny side inwards. Make gravy in the roasting tin and heat any vegetables in the microwave while doing so. Use the cooking water from boiled vegetables along with stock to make the gravy.

* The pudding can be left boiling while the starter and main courses are eaten but do remember to check the water level before sitting down to eat.

Thawing the Turkey

Always allow sufficient time for thawing the turkey in the refrigerator before cooking. Unwrap the bird and place it in a covered deep dish in the refrigerator, preferably on a low shelf, ensuring that it will not drip on any other food. Occasionally, drain off the liquid which seeps from the turkey as it thaws.

The following is a guide to recommended thawing times by weight in the refrigerator: these times are not exact and they can only act as a guide. As soon as it is possible to do so, remove the giblets, and cook them to make stock. Cool the stock and freeze it until required. This is preferable to storing the stock in the refrigerator for several days while the turkey continues to thaw.

Roasting the Turkey

Turkey requires long, slow cooking to ensure that the meat is thoroughly cooked. This is particularly important if the body cavity has been stuffed.

Place the bird in a roasting tin, using a rack or trivet if liked. Brush with a little melted butter or oil if required and sprinkle with seasoning (see individual recipes for more detailed information). Cover the breast with streaky bacon to prevent the meat from drying out. Additionally, turkey should be covered with foil for part of the cooking time to prevent over-browning. Turn the bird several times, basting it each time, to promote moist, even cooking.

The following times, at 180°C/350°F/gas 4, are a guide only, based upon the bird's weight **excluding** the stuffing, since it is not easy to weigh a stuffed turkey. Birds without stuffing will take slightly less time to cook. To test, pierce the meat at a thick part - for example on the thigh behind the drumstick. Check for any signs of blood in the juices and for any meat that appears pink or uncooked. When the bird is cooked, the juices will run clear and the meat will be firm and white right through to the bone. On a large bird, test in at least two places to ensure that all the meat is well cooked.

WEIGHT OF TURKEY	THAWING TIME IN REFRIGERATOR
2.5-3.5 kg/5½-8 lb	up to 2 days
3.5-5.5 kg/8-12 lb	2½ to 3 days
5.5-7.25 kg/12-16 lb	3-4 days
7.25-9 kg/16-20 lb	4-4½ days

WEIGHT (BEFORE STUFFING)	ROASTING TIME AT 180°C/350°F/GAS 4
2.5 kg/5 lb	2½-3 hours
2.75-3.5 kg/6-8 lb	3-3¾ hours
3.5-4.5 kg/8-10 lb	3¾-4½ hours
4.5-5.5 kg/10-12 lb	4½-5 hours
5.5-11.4 kg/12-25 lb	20 minutes per 450g/1 lb plus 20 minutes

Mrs Beeton's Roast Turkey

ILLUSTRATED ON PAGE 79

The recipe that follows is based upon a 6 kg/13 lb bird.
Timings for birds of different weights are on page 81.

fat for basting
1 turkey
450 g/1 lb Mrs Beeton's Forcemeat (right)
675 g/1½ lb seasoned sausagemeat
225 g/8 oz rindless streaky bacon rashers

Set the oven at 220°C/425°F/gas 7. Weigh the turkey. Trim it, and wash it inside and out in cold water. Pat dry with absorbent kitchen paper. Immediately before cooking, stuff the neck of the bird with forcemeat. Put the sausagemeat inside the body cavity. Cover the breast of the bird with the bacon rashers.

Place the prepared turkey in a roasting tin. Cover with foil and roast for 15 minutes. Lower the oven temperature to 180°C/350°F/gas 4 and roast for 20 minutes per 450 g/1 lb (unstuffed weight) plus 20 minutes, or until cooked through. Remove the foil for the last hour of cooking and the bacon strips for the final 20 minutes to allow the breast to brown.

Serve on a heated platter, with roasted or grilled chipolata sausages, bacon rolls (see page 44) and bread sauce.

SERVES FOURTEEN TO SIXTEEN

MRS BEETON'S TIP
Lemons, cut in half and with all flesh and pulp removed, make ideal containers for individual portions of cranberry sauce. Arrange them around the turkey.

Mrs Beeton's Forcemeat

ILLUSTRATED ON PAGE 79

100 g/4 oz gammon or rindless bacon, finely chopped
50 g/2 oz shredded beef suet
grated rind of 1 lemon
5 ml/1 tsp chopped parsley
5 ml/1 tsp chopped mixed herbs
salt and cayenne pepper
pinch of ground mace
150 g/5 oz fresh white breadcrumbs
2 eggs, lightly beaten

Combine the gammon or bacon, suet, lemon rind and herbs in a bowl. Add salt, cayenne and mace to taste, mix well with a fork, then stir in the breadcrumbs. Gradually add enough beaten egg to bind.

MAKES ABOUT 350 G/12 OZ

VARIATION

Mrs Beeton's Forcemeat Balls Roll the mixture into 6-8 small balls. Either cook the forcemeat balls around a roast joint or bird, or fry them in a little oil until browned and cooked through.

Sage and Onion Stuffing

ILLUSTRATED ON PAGE 79

4 onions, thickly sliced
8 young fresh sage sprigs or 20 ml/4 tsp dried sage
225 g/8 oz fresh white breadcrumbs
100 g/4 oz butter or margarine, melted
salt and pepper
1-2 eggs, lightly beaten

Put the onions in a small saucepan with water to cover. Bring to the boil, cook for 2-3 minutes, then remove the onions from the pan with a slotted spoon. Chop them finely. Chop the sage leaves finely, discarding any stalk.

Combine the breadcrumbs, onions and sage in a bowl. Add the melted butter or margarine, with salt and pepper to taste. Mix well, moistening the stuffing with a little of the beaten egg. If the stuffing is to be shaped into balls, bind it with the beaten egg.

SUFFICIENT FOR 1 (4-5 KG/9-11 LB) GOOSE; USE HALF FOR
1(2.5 KG/5½ LB) DUCK

CHESTNUT STUFFING

ILLUSTRATED ON PAGE 79

800 g/1 lb chestnuts, shelled (see Nesselrode Pudding 53)
150-250 ml/5-8 fl oz chicken or vegetable stock
50 g/2 oz butter, softened
pinch of ground cinnamon
2.5 ml/½ tsp sugar
salt and pepper

Put the shelled chestnuts in a saucepan and add the stock. Bring to the boil, lower the heat, cover and simmer until the chestnuts are tender. Drain, reserving the stock.

Rub the chestnuts through a fine wire sieve into a bowl. Add the butter, cinnamon and sugar, with salt and pepper to taste. Stir in enough of the reserved stock to bind.

SUFFICIENT FOR THE NECK END OF 1 (5-6 KG/9-11 LB)
TURKEY; USE HALF FOR 1 (1.5 KG/3 LB) CHICKEN

BREAD SAUCE

600 ml/1 pint milk
1 large onion studded with 6 cloves
1 blade of mace
4 peppercorns
1 allspice berry
1 bay leaf
100 g/4 oz fine fresh white breadcrumbs
15 ml/1 tbsp butter
salt and pepper
freshly grated nutmeg
30 ml/2 tbsp single cream (optional)

Put the milk in a small saucepan with the studded onion, mace, peppercorns, allspice and bay leaf. Bring very slowly to boiling point, then remove from the heat, cover the pan and set it aside for 30 minutes to infuse.

Strain the flavoured milk into a heatproof bowl, pressing the onion against the sides of the strainer to extract as much of the liquid as possible. Stir in the breadcrumbs and butter, with salt, pepper and nutmeg to taste.

Set the bowl over simmering water and cook for 20 minutes, stirring occasionally until thick and creamy. Stir in the cream, if using, just before serving the sauce.

MAKES ABOUT 250 ML/8 FL OZ

MRS BEETON'S TIP
Canned chestnuts may be used for the stuffing.
You will require about 450 g/1 lb.

MICROWAVE TIP
There is no need to infuse the onion in the milk if the sauce is to be made in the microwave. Simply put the clove-studded onion in a deep bowl, cover and cook on High for 2 minutes. Add the spices, bay leaf and milk, cover loosely and cook on High for 6-6½ minutes. Stir in the remaining ingredients, except the cream, and cook for 2 minutes more. Remove the studded onion, whole spices and bay leaf. Whisk the sauce, adding the cream if liked.

CHESTNUT SAUCE

Serve this creamy sauce instead of chestnut stuffing with turkey. It also goes well with roast, grilled or pan-fried chicken.

225 g/8 oz chestnuts, shelled (see Nesselrode Pudding page 53)
300 ml/½ pint chicken stock
2 strips of lemon rind
salt and pepper
cayenne pepper
150 ml/¼ pint single cream
lemon juice

Put the shelled chestnuts in a pan and add the stock and lemon rind. Bring to the boil, lower the heat and simmer for 15 minutes.

Pure the chestnuts with the stock in a blender or food processor, or press through a fine sieve into a clean pan. Add salt, pepper and cayenne to taste. Stir in the cream and heat through without boiling. Add lemon juice to taste to sharpen the sauce. Serve.

MAKES ABOUT 600 ML/1 PINT

 RAVY

Add a few drops of Christopher North's Sauce (page 26) to heighten the flavour. Alternatively, add 60 ml/4 tbsp port or sherry, and 15 ml/1 tbsp redcurrant jelly to make a rich gravy for duck or goose.

giblets, carcass bones or trimmings from meat, poultry or game
1 bay leaf
1 thyme sprig
1 clove
6 black peppercorns
1 onion, sliced
pan juices from roasting (see Mrs Beeton's Tip)
25 g/1 oz plain flour (optional)
salt and pepper

Place the giblets, bones, carcass and/or trimmings (for example wing ends) in a saucepan. Pour in water to cover, then add the bay leaf, thyme, clove, peppercorns and onion. Bring to the boil and skim off any scum, then lower the heat, cover the pan and simmer for about 1 hour.

Strain the stock and measure it. You need about 600-750 ml/1-1¼ pints to make gravy for up to six servings. If necessary, pour the stock back into the saucepan and boil until reduced.

Pour off most of the fat from the roasting tin, leaving a thin layer and all the cooking juices. Place the tin over moderate heat; add the flour if the gravy is to be thickened. Cook the flour, stirring all the time and scraping all the sediment off the tin, for about 3 minutes, until it is browned. If the gravy is not thickened, pour in about 300 ml/½ pint of the stock and boil, stirring and scraping, until the sediment on the base of the tin is incorporated.

Slowly pour in the stock (or the remaining stock, if making thin gravy), stirring all the time. Bring to the boil and cook for 2-3 minutes to reduce the gravy and concentrate the flavour slightly. Taste and add more salt and pepper if required.

SERVES FOUR TO SIX

MRS BEETON'S TIP

The quality of the sediment on the base of the cooking tin determines the quality of the gravy. If the meat was well seasoned and roasted until well browned outside, the sediment should have a good colour and flavour. Any herbs (other than large stalks), onions or flavouring roasted under the meat should be left in the pan until the gravy is boiled, then strained out before serving.

CRANBERRY SAUCE

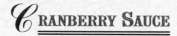

Illustrated on page 79

150 g/5 oz sugar
225 g/8 oz cranberries

Put the sugar in a heavy-bottomed saucepan. Add 125 ml/4 fl oz water. Stir over gentle heat until the sugar dissolves. Add the cranberries and cook gently for about 10 minutes until they have burst and are quite tender. Leave to cool.

MAKES ABOUT 300 ML/½ PINT

VARIATIONS

Cranberry and Apple Use half cranberries and half tart cooking apples.
Cranberry and Orange Use orange juice instead of water. Add 10 ml/2 tsp finely grated orange rind.
Cranberry and Sherry Add 30-45 ml/2-3 tbsp sherry with the cranberries.

BROWN APPLE SAUCE

In Mrs Beeton's day, this tangy, apple-flavoured gravy was frequently served as an accompaniment to goose or roast pork. It is also suitable for grilled pork or gammon.

350 g/12 oz Bramley apples
300 ml/½ pint Gravy (page 84) made with poultry or pork cooking juices
45 ml/3 tbsp sugar
salt and pepper · cayenne pepper

Quarter, peel, core and slice the apples. Put them in a saucepan with the gravy. Bring to the boil, reduce the heat and cover the pan. Simmer for 10-15 minutes until the apple is reduced to a pulp. Beat the pulp into the gravy until smooth. Add the sugar with salt, pepper and cayenne to taste. Serve hot.

MAKES ABOUT 600 ML/1 PINT

ROAST GOOSE WITH STUFFING AND RED CABBAGE

ILLUSTRATED ON PAGE 87

1 goose with giblets
½ lemon · salt and pepper
350 g/12 oz prunes, soaked overnight in water to cover
450 g/1 lb cooking apples
15 ml/1 tbsp redcurrant jelly

RED CABBAGE
50 g/2 oz butter
1.5 kg/3¼ lb red cabbage, finely shredded
50 g/2 oz demerara sugar
75 ml/5 tbsp malt or cider vinegar

Put the giblets from the goose in a saucepan. Add 1.5 litres/2¾ pints water and bring to the boil. Simmer until the liquid is reduced by half. Strain. Set the oven at 230°C/450°F/gas 8. Weigh the goose and calculate the cooking time at 20 minutes per 450 g/1 lb. Remove the excess fat usually found around the vent. Rinse the inside of the bird, then rub the skin with lemon. Season with salt and pepper.

Drain the prunes, remove the stones and roughly chop the flesh. Peel, core and chop the apples. Add them to the prunes, with salt and pepper. Use the mixture to stuff the bird. Put the goose on a rack in a roasting tin. Place in the oven; lower the temperature to 180°C/350°F/gas 4. Cook for the calculated time. Drain fat from the tin occasionally.

Meanwhile, melt the butter in a large flame-proof casserole, add the red cabbage and sugar and stir well. Pour in 75 ml/5 tbsp water and the vinegar, with salt and pepper to taste. Cover and cook in the oven for about 2 hours, stirring occasionally.

When the goose is cooked, transfer it to a heated serving platter and keep hot. Drain off the excess fat from the roasting tin, retaining the juices. Stir in the reserved giblet stock and cook over fairly high heat until reduced to a thin gravy. Stir in the redcurrant jelly. Serve the gravy and red cabbage separately.

SERVES SIX TO EIGHT

ROAST RIBS OF BEEF WITH YORKSHIRE PUDDING

This impressive joint is also known as a standing rib roast. Ask the butcher to trim the thin ends of the bones so that the joint will stand upright. The recipe below, as in Mrs Beeton's day, uses clarified dripping for cooking, but the roast may be cooked without any additional fat, if preferred. There will be sufficient fat from the meat for basting.

2.5 kg/5½ lb forerib of beef
50-75 g/2-3 oz beef dripping
salt and pepper
vegetable stock or water (see method)

YORKSHIRE PUDDING
100 g/4 oz plain flour
1 egg, beaten
150 ml/¼ pint milk

Set the oven at 230°C/450°F/gas 8. Wipe the meat but do not salt it. Melt 50 g/2 oz of the dripping in a roasting tin, add the meat and quickly spoon some of the hot fat over it. Roast for 10 minutes.

Turn the oven temperature down to 180°C/350°F/gas 4. Baste the meat thoroughly, then continue to roast for a further 1¾ hours for rare meat; 2 hours for well-done meat. Baste frequently during cooking.

Meanwhile make the Yorkshire pudding batter. Sift the flour into a bowl and add a pinch of salt. Make a well in the centre of the flour and add the beaten egg. Stir in the milk, gradually working in the flour. Beat vigorously until the mixture is smooth and bubbly, then stir in 150 ml/¼ pint water.

About 30 minutes before the end of the cooking time, spoon off 30 ml/2 tbsp of the dripping and divide it between six 7.5 cm/3 inch Yorkshire pudding tins. Place the tins in the oven for 5 minutes or until the fat is very hot, then carefully divide the batter between them. Bake above the meat for 15-20 minutes.

When the beef is cooked, salt it lightly, transfer it to a warmed serving platter and keep hot. Pour off almost all the water in the roasting tin, leaving the sediment. Pour in enough vegetable stock or water to make a thin gravy, then heat to boiling point, stirring all the time. Season with salt and pepper and serve in a gravyboat with the roast and Yorkshire puddings

SERVES SIX TO EIGHT

MRS BEETON'S TIP
Yorkshire pudding is traditionally cooked in a large tin below the joint, so that some of the cooking juices from the meat fall into the pudding to give it an excellent flavour. In a modern oven, this means using a rotisserie or resting the meat directly on the oven shelf. The pudding should be cooked in a large roasting tin, then cut into portions and served as a course on its own before the meat course. Gravy should be poured over the portions of pudding.

HORSERADISH SAUCE

60 ml/4 tbsp grated horseradish
5 ml/1 tsp caster sugar
5 ml/1 tsp salt
2.5 ml/½ tsp pepper
10 ml/2 tsp prepared mustard
malt vinegar (see method)
45-60/3-4 tbsp single cream (optional)

Mix the horseradish, sugar, salt, pepper and mustard in a non-metallic bowl. Stir in enough vinegar to make a sauce with the consistency of cream. The flavour and appearance will be improved if the quantity of vinegar is reduced, and the cream added.

MAKES ABOUT 150 ML/¼ PINT

*Roast Goose with Stuffing and Red Cabbage (page 85),
garnished with kumquats and bay leaves*

ROASTING TIMES FOR BEEF AND PORK

The following times are a guide for roasting meat at 180°C/350°/gas 4. Weights and timings are for oven-ready joints, including any stuffing. Small joints weighing less than 1 kg/2¼ lb may need an extra 5 minutes per 450 g/ 1 lb.

Personal preferences play an important role when roasting, and there are many methods. For example, the joint may be placed in an oven preheated to a higher temperature than that recommended for general roasting. The temperature may be reduced immediately or after the first 5-15 minutes. This method is popular for pork (to crisp the rind) and for sealing and browning the outside of larger joints of beef. Small to medium joints may need less time than that calculated below, if they are started off at a high temperature, but thick or large joints will still require the full calculated time to ensure they are cooked.

Attitudes towards roasting pork have changed considerably, based on professional guidance on food safety. Pork is usually served cooked through, not rare or medium; however, the meat may be roasted until it is succulent rather than very dry; hence the choice of two recommended timings.

Beef

Rare	20 minutes per 450 g/1 lb plus 20 minutes
Medium	20 minutes per 450 g/1 lb plus 25 minutes
Well done	30 minutes per 450 g/1 lb plus 30 minutes

Pork

Medium	20-25 minutes per 450 g/1 lb plus 25-30 minutes
Well Done	25-30 minutes per 450 g/1 lb

USING A MEAT THERMOMETER

A meat thermometer may be inserted into the joint before cooking, ready to register the internal temperature and indicate the extent of cooking. Preheat the thermometer in the oven from cold. Pierce the meat at the thickest point with a skewer and insert the hot thermometer into it. At any stage during cooking the reading on the thermometer may be checked to assess cooking progress (see chart below). When the meat is cooked, remove the thermometer and place it on a plate to cool.

Beef

Rare	60°C/140°F
Medium	70°C/158°F
Well done	80°C/176°F

Pork

Medium	75°-80°C/167°-176°F
Well Done	80°-85°C/176°-185°F

CARVING A SIRLOIN OF BEEF

To carve a sirloin on the bone, first cut out the fillet or under-cut and carve it into slices.

Then turn the sirloin over, so that it rests on the bone, and carve the meat across the width of the joint and straight down towards the blade of the bone. These slices are thicker than those from a boneless joint.

To carve a boned and rolled sirloin, cut a thick slice first from the outside of the joint leaving the surface smooth; then carve thin, even slices.

'The Baron of Beef - This noble joint, which consisted of two sirloins not cut asunder, was a favourite dish of our ancestors. It is rarely seen nowadays; indeed, it seems out of place on a modern table, as it requires the grim boar's head and Christmas pie as supporters. Sir Walter Scott has described a feast at which the baron of beef would have appeared to great advantage. We will quote a few lines to remind us of those days when "England was merry England," and when hospitality was thought to be the highest virtue."

"The fire, with well-dried logs supplied,
Went roaring up the chimney wide;
The huge hall-table's oaken face,
Scrubb'd till it shone, the day to grace,
Bore then, upon its massive board,
No mark to part the squire and lord.
Then was brought in the lusty brawn,
By old blue-coated serving-man;
Then the grim boar's head frown'd on high,
Crested with bays and rosemary.
Well can the green-garb'd ranger tell
How, when, and where the monster fell;
What dogs before his death he tore,
And all the baiting of the boar;
While round the merry wassel bowl,
Garnish'd with ribbons, blithe did trowl.
There the huge sirloin reek'd; hard by
Plum-porridge stood, and Christmas pie;
Nor rail'd old Scotland to produce,
At such high tide, her savoury goose.'

MRS BEETON (1861)

CARVING A TURKEY

As Mrs Beeton noted in her Book of Household Management (1861), the only art in carving a turkey consists 'in getting from the breast as many fine slices as possible; and all must have remarked the very great difference in the large number of people whom a good carver will find slices for, and the comparatively few that a bad carver will succeed in serving.'

1 Insert a carving fork firmly in the breast of the bird. On each side, make a downward cut with a sharp knife between the thigh and the body, then turn the blade outwards so that the joint is exposed. Cut through it with either poultry shears or a sharp carving knife. Put the legs to one side.
2 With the fork still inserted in the breast, remove the wings by cutting widely, but not too deeply, over the adjacent part of the breast, to give the wing enough meat without depriving the breast of too much flesh.
3 The breast can be sliced from the carcass as a whole. Alternatively, it can be separated from the back by cutting through the rib bones with poultry shears or a sharp knife.

Carve the brown meat off the legs, if liked, working downwards in thin slices, following the direction of the bone. Serve both white and dark meat to each person, together with a portion of each of the stuffings.

To complete the carving of a large bird whose breast and back have been separated, place the back on the dish with the rib bones facing downwards; press the knife firmly across the centre of it, and raise the neck end at the same time with the fork to divide the back into two.
4 Remove the two 'oysters' (choice morsels of dark-coloured flesh) from the shallow hollows beside the thigh sockets. To do this, the tail part of the back must be stood on end and held firmly with the fork.

BRUSSELS SPROUTS WITH CHESTNUTS

ILLUSTRATED ON PAGE 79

This is a classic accompaniment to the Christmas turkey. The slightly sweet flavour of the chestnuts is the perfect foil for the Brussels sprouts.

225 g/8 oz chestnuts, shelled (see Nesselrode Pudding, page 53)
1 kg/2¼ lb Brussels sprouts
75 g/3 oz cooked ham, finely chopped
60 ml/4 tbsp single cream · salt and pepper

Set the oven at 180°C/350°F/gas 4. Place the cleaned nuts in a saucepan, just cover with water and bring to the boil. Cover the pan, lower the heat, and simmer for about 20 minutes or until the nuts are tender. Drain, then cut each chestnut into quarters.

Trim the sprouts, pulling off any damaged leaves. Using a sharp knife, cut a cross in the base of each. Cook the sprouts in a saucepan of salted boiling water for 5-10 minutes until just tender. Drain well.

Combine the sprouts, chestnuts and ham in a small casserole. Stir in the cream and season with salt and pepper. Cover and bake for 15 minutes.

SERVES SIX

BRAISED CHESTNUTS WITH ONION AND CELERY

ILLUSTRATED ON PAGE 95

600 ml/1 pint beef stock
1 kg/2¼ lb chestnuts, peeled (see Nesselrode Pudding, page 53)
1 small onion stuck with 2 cloves
3 celery sticks, roughly chopped
1 bay leaf
1 blade of mace
pinch of cayenne pepper · salt
puff pastry fleurons (see Mrs Beeton's Tip, page 97)

Bring the stock to the boil in a saucepan. Add the chestnuts, onion, celery, bay leaf, mace and cayenne, with a little salt. Cover and simmer for about 30 minutes, until the nuts are tender.

Drain the chestnuts, reserving the cooking liquid, and keep them hot in a serving dish. Chop the onion, discarding the cloves, and add it to the chestnuts. Discard the bay leaf and mace. Return the cooking liquid to the clean pan. Boil the liquid rapidly until it is reduced to a thin glaze. Pour the glaze over the chestnuts and garnish with the fleurons.

SERVES SIX

BRAISED CELERY

ILLUSTRATED ON PAGE 79

15 ml/1 tbsp dripping or margarine
2 rindless bacon rashers, chopped
2 onions, finely chopped
1 carrot, finely chopped
½ turnip, finely chopped
chicken stock (see method)
4 celery hearts, washed but left whole
15 ml/1 tbsp chopped fresh coriander or parsley

Melt the dripping or margarine in a large heavy-bottomed saucepan. Add the bacon and fry for 2 minutes, then stir in the onions, carrot and turnip. Cook over gentle heat, stirring occasionally, for 10 minutes.

Pour over enough chicken stock to half cover the vegetables. Place the celery on top and spoon over some of the stock. Cover the pan tightly with foil and a lid and cook over very gentle heat for 1 hours or until the celery is very tender. Baste the celery occasionally with the stock.

Using a slotted spoon, transfer the celery to a heated serving dish. Drain the cooking liquid into a small pan, reserving the mirepoix. Boil the cooking liquid rapidly until it is reduced to a thin glaze, then pour it over the celery. Sprinkle the mirepoix with the chopped coriander or parsley and serve it as a separate vegetable dish.

SERVES FOUR

Vegetarian Main Dishes

Boston Roast

fat for greasing
300 g/11 oz haricot beans, soaked overnight
salt and pepper · 15 ml/1 tbsp oil
1 onion, chopped
150 g/5 oz Cheddar cheese, grated
60 ml/4 tbsp vegetable stock
1 egg, beaten
100 g/4 oz fresh white breadcrumbs
5 ml/1 tsp dried thyme
2.5 ml/½ tsp grated nutmeg

Drain the beans, put them in a saucepan and add fresh water to cover. Do not add salt. Boil for 10 minutes, then lower the heat and simmer for about 40 minutes or until tender. Drain the beans. Mash with seasoning or purée in a food processor.

Set the oven at 180°C/350°F/gas 4. Heat the oil in a frying pan, add the onion and fry for about 10 minutes, or until softened. Mix with the beans and remaining ingredients.

Spoon the mixture into a well-greased 900 g/2 lb loaf tin. Cover the surface with greased greaseproof paper. Bake for 45 minutes, until firm and slightly shrunk. Serve with Ratatouille (page 107).

SERVES SIX

Buckwheat Bake

fat for greasing
200 g/7 oz roasted buckwheat
1 egg · 75 g/3 oz butter
salt and pepper
75 g/3 oz Parmesan cheese, grated

Grease a 900 ml/1½ pint baking dish. Set the oven at 190°C/375°F/gas 5. Put the buckwheat into a large saucepan with 600 ml/1 pint cold water. Bring to the boil, lower the heat to the lowest setting and cover the pan tightly. Leave for 15 minutes, by which time the grains should have absorbed the liquid.

Tip the buckwheat into a bowl, add the egg and beat well. Stir in 25 g/1 oz of the butter and seasoning. Melt the remaining butter. Layer the buckwheat and cheese in the dish. Pour the remaining butter over. Bake for 20-30 minutes.

SERVES THREE TO FOUR

Semolina Gnocchi

ILLUSTRATED ON PAGE 95

fat for greasing
500 ml/17 fl oz milk
100 g/4 oz semolina
salt and pepper
1.25 ml/¼ tsp grated nutmeg · 1 egg
100 g/4 oz Parmesan cheese, grated
25 g/1 oz butter

Grease a shallow ovenproof dish. Bring the milk to the boil in a saucepan. Sprinkle in the semolina and stir over low heat until thick. Mix in the salt, pepper, nutmeg, egg and 75 g/3 oz of the Parmesan. Beat until smooth. Spread on a shallow dish and cool.

Set the oven at 200°C/400°F/gas 6, if using. Cut the semolina into 2 cm/¾ inch squares or rounds. Place in the prepared dish and sprinkle with the remaining Parmesan; dot with butter. Brown under the grill or in the oven for 8-10 minutes.

SERVES FOUR

MRS BEETON'S TIP

Canned chopped tomatoes make a quick sauce. Add them to a chopped onion cooked in butter or oil until soft. Simmer for 5 minutes, then add salt, pepper and plenty of chopped parsley. Herbs, such as bay and marjoram, and garlic may be added; with a little red wine and longer simmering the sauce is rich and excellent.

MINCEMEAT MERINGUE PIE

ILLUSTRATED PAGE 95

To save time, the pie can be cooked in advance, up to the stage when the breadcrumb filling is baked in the flan case. Add the mincemeat and meringue topping and finish cooking just before serving.

50 g/2 oz soft white breadcrumbs
30 ml/2 tbsp granulated sugar
2 eggs, separated
375 ml/13 fl oz milk
15 ml/1 tbsp butter
2.5 ml/½ tsp vanilla essence
225 g/8 oz mincemeat
75 g/3 oz caster sugar

SHORT CRUST PASTRY
100 g/4 oz plain flour
2.5 ml/½ tsp salt
50 g/2 oz margarine (or half butter, half lard)
flour for rolling out

Make the short crust pasty, following the instructions in Mrs Beeton's Apple Flan (page 56). Set the oven at 200°C/400°F/gas 6.

Roll out the pastry on a lightly floured surface and use to line an 18 cm/7 inch flan tin or ring placed on a baking sheet. Line the pastry with greaseproof paper and fill with baking beans. Bake 'blind' for 10 minutes, then remove the paper and beans. Return to the oven for 5 minutes, then remove. Lower the oven temperature to 180°C/350°F/gas 4.

Combine the breadcrumbs, sugar and egg yolks in a bowl and mix well. Warm the milk and butter together in a saucepan until the butter has just melted, then stir slowly into the breadcrumb mixture. Mix well, then stir in the vanilla essence. Leave to stand for 5 minutes.

Pour the breadcrumb filling into the flan case and bake for 35-45 minutes or until the custard is firm. Remove from the oven. Turn the oven temperature up to 200°C/400°F/gas 6. Spread the mincemeat over the crumb custard. Whisk the egg whites in a clean, grease-free bowl until stiff, gradually whisking in about 50 g/2 oz of the caster sugar. Pile or spoon the meringue over the pie filling, covering both the mincemeat and the pastry edge completely. Sprinkle with the remaining sugar. Bake for 5-10 minutes until the meringue is golden. Serve at once, with cream.

SERVES FOUR TO SIX

PLUM PUDDING SAUCE

A thin sauce with a rich, buttery flavour to make a potent impression on Christmas pudding.

100 g/4 oz caster sugar
75 ml/3 fl oz brandy
50 g/2 oz unsalted butter, diced
175 ml/6 fl oz Madeira

Put the sugar in a heatproof bowl with 30 ml/2 tbsp of the brandy. Add the butter. Set over simmering water and stir until the mixture is smooth. Gradually stir in the rest of the brandy with the Madeira and warm through. Either serve over the pudding or in a sauceboat.

MAKES 350 ML/12 FL OZ

SWEET WHITE SAUCE

20 ml/4 tsp cornflour
250 ml/8 fl oz milk
15-30 ml/1-2 tbsp sugar
vanilla essence or other flavouring

Put the cornflour in a bowl. Stir in enough of the cold milk to form a smooth, thin paste. Heat the remaining milk in a small saucepan. When it boils, stir it into the cornflour paste, then return the mixture to the clean pan and stir until boiling. Lower the heat and cook, stirring frequently, for 3 minutes. Stir in sugar to taste. Add the chosen flavouring. Serve hot.

MAKES ABOUT 250 ML/8 FL OZ

VARIATION

Brandy Sauce When the sauce is cooked, stir in 15-30 ml/1-2 tbsp brandy.

Orange Sauce When the sauce is cooked, stir in the grated rind of 1 orange. Add 30 ml/2 tbsp orange liqueur, if liked.

Rum and Almond Sauce When the sauce is cooked, stir in 30 ml/2 tbsp white rum and a few drops of almond essence.

Mrs Beeton's Trifle

ILLUSTRATED ON PAGE 99

Plain whisked or creamed sponge cake, individual buns, or Madeira cake are ideal for this trifle. Originally, Mrs Beeton made her custard by using 8 eggs to thicken 600 ml/1 pint milk, cooking it slowly over hot water. Using cornflour and egg yolks is more practical and it gives a creamier, less 'eggy' result.

4 slices of plain cake or individual cakes
6 almond macaroons
12 ratafias · 175 ml/6 fl oz sherry
30-45 ml/2-3 tbsp brandy
60-90 ml/4-6 tbsp raspberry or strawberry jam
grated rind of ½ lemon
25 g/1 oz flaked almonds
300 ml/½ pint double cream
30 ml/2 tbsp icing sugar
candied and crystallized fruit and peel to decorate

CUSTARD
25 g/1 oz cornflour
25 g/1 oz caster sugar
4 egg yolks · 5 ml/1 tsp vanilla essence
600 ml/1 pint milk

Place the sponge cakes in a glass dish. Add the macaroons and ratafias, pressing them down gently. Pour about 50 ml/2 fl oz of the sherry into a bowl and set it aside, then pour the rest over the biscuits and cake. Sprinkle with the brandy. Warm the jam in a small saucepan, then pour it evenly over the trifle base. Top with the lemon rind and almonds.

For the custard, blend the cornflour, caster sugar, egg yolks and vanilla to a smooth cream with a little of the milk. Heat the remaining milk until hot. Pour some of the milk on to the egg mixture, stirring, then replace the mixture in the saucepan with the rest of the milk. Bring to the boil, stirring constantly, then simmer for 3 minutes. Pour the custard over the trifle base and cover the surface with a piece of dampened greaseproof paper. Set aside to cool.

Add the cream and icing sugar to the reserved sherry and whip until the mixture stands in soft peaks. Swirl the cream over the top of the trifle and chill. Decorate with pieces of candied and crystallized fruit and peel before serving.

SERVES SIX

Vanilla Custard

10 ml/2 tsp cornflour
500 ml/17 fl oz milk
25 g/1 oz caster sugar
2 eggs · vanilla essence

In a bowl, mix the cornflour to a smooth paste with a little of the cold milk. Heat the rest of the milk in a saucepan and when hot pour it on to the blended cornflour, stirring. Return the mixture to the pan, bring to the boil, and boil for 1-2 minutes, stirring all the time, to cook the cornflour. Remove from the heat and stir in the sugar. Leave to cool.

Beat the eggs together lightly in a small bowl. Add a little of the cooked cornflour mixture, stir well, then pour into the pan. Heat gently for a few minutes until the custard has thickened, stirring all the time. Do not boil. Stir in a few drops of vanilla essence. Serve hot or cold.

MAKES ABOUT 600 ML/1 PINT

BOXING DAY

The Boxing Day buffet is traditionally laden with cold meats, complemented by a good choice of pickles, and intended for informal family dining. A hot dish of haricot beans and tempting salads complete both vegetarian meals or the cold meat platters. Simple prepare-ahead desserts or the classic fruit and nut bowl will fulfil the victualling requirements.

BOILED DRESSED HAM

1 leg of ham
250 ml/8 fl oz cider or white wine (optional)
1 large onion, roughly chopped
3-4 celery sticks, roughly chopped
1 large turnip, roughly chopped
1 large carrot, roughly chopped
1 bouquet garni

GARNISH
browned breadcrumbs
demerara sugar
cloves
small bunches of watercress

Weigh the ham. Depending on how salty the ham is, it may be necessary to soak it in cold water for up to 12 hours. Soaking is not usually necessary with modern curing, however, since less salt is used. Check with your butcher.

Drain the ham if necessary. Place it in a large saucepan, cover with fresh water and bring to the boil. Skim off any scum that rises to the surface, lower the heat and simmer for 20 minutes per 450 g/1 lb, or until the bone at the knuckle end sticks out about 2.5 cm/1 inch and starts to feel loose.

Pour off the water from the pan and add the cider or wine, if used. Add fresh tepid water to cover, together with the prepared vegetables and bouquet garni. Bring the liquid to simmering point, half cover the pan and simmer gently for 10 minutes per 450 g/1 lb.

When the ham is cooked, lift it out of the pan. Remove the rind and score the fat into a diamond pattern, using a sharp knife and making the cuts about 5 mm/¼ inch deep.

Cover the fat with equal quantities of browned breadcrumbs and demerara sugar. Press a clove into the centre of each diamond pattern. Place small bunches of watercress at either end of the ham and cover the knuckle with a pie frill. Serve hot or cold.

MRS BEETON'S TIP
Whole hams vary considerably in size and in the relation of meat to bone. It is therefore difficult to give exact servings. As a general guide, a 4.5 kg/10 lb ham should feed 30 people.

A Vegetarian Christmas Dinner: Ratatouille (page 107); Semolina Gnocchi (page 91) with Braised Chestnuts with Onion and Celery (page 90) buttered sprouts and carrots; and Mincemeat Meringue Pie (page 92)

PORK CHEESE

Originally presented as an excellent breakfast dish, this pâté style recipe for cooked pork may be served with bread or toast and a salad. Scoop it out of the baking dish rather than attempt to unmould the mixture or bottom-line the dish with greased greaseproof paper to turn out and slice the pork cheese.

1.4 kg/3 lb belly of pork, boned
salt and pepper
30 ml/2 tbsp chopped parsley
5 ml/1 tsp chopped fresh thyme or 2.5 ml/½ tsp dried thyme
2.5 ml/½ tsp chopped rosemary
15 ml/1 tbsp chopped fresh sage or 5 ml/1 tsp dried sage
2.5 ml/½ tsp ground mace
a little grated nutmeg
grated rind of ½ lemon
300 ml/½ pint pork gravy (see Mrs Beeton's Tip)
butter for greasing

Set the oven at 180°C/350°F/gas 4. Place the pork in a roasting tin and cook for 1½ hours, until cooked through. Leave to cool for about 30 minutes, or until the meat is just cool enough to handle.

Set the oven at 180°C/350°F/gas 4 again. Use a sharp paring knife or fine-bladed knife to cut all the rind off the pork. Chop the meat and fat, either by hand or in a food processor. Do not overprocess the mixture as the pieces should resemble very fine dice. Place the pork in a large bowl. Add plenty of salt and pepper, all the herbs, the mace, nutmeg and lemon rind. If you have a large pestle, then use it to pound the meat with the flavouring ingredients; if not, use the back of a sturdy mixing spoon. The more you pound the mixture, the better the texture.

When all the ingredients are thoroughly mixed, work in the gravy to bind them together loosely. Good thick gravy is best as it will not make the mixture too runny, more can be incorporated and the cheese will have a good flavour.

Grease a 1.1 litre/2 pint ovenproof dish, for example a soufflé dish or terrine. Turn the mixture into the dish, smooth it down and cover with foil.

Bake for 1¼ hours, then leave to cool completely. Chill overnight before serving.

SERVES TEN TO TWELVE

MRS BEETON'S TIP

After roasting the pork, pour off excess fat, then use the cooking juices to make gravy. Allow 40 g/1 oz plain flour to 600 ml/1 pint chicken or vegetable stock. Stir the flour into the residue in the roasting tin and cook, stirring, for 3 minutes. Gradually stir in the stock, bring to

---

HARICOT BEANS WITH ONION AND CARAWAY

200 g/7 oz haricot beans, soaked overnight in cold water to cover
25 g/1 oz butter
2 onions, finely chopped
5 ml/1 tsp caraway seeds
salt and pepper
125 ml/4 fl oz soured cream
30 ml/2 tbsp chopped parsley

Drain the beans. Put them in a saucepan with fresh water to cover. Bring to the boil, boil vigorously for 10 minutes, then lower the heat, cover the pan and simmer for about 40 minutes or until the beans are tender. Drain thoroughly.

Melt the butter in a saucepan. Add the onions and caraway seeds and fry for about 10 minutes until just transparent. Add the beans, with salt and pepper to taste, and toss together until heated through.

Spoon into a heated serving dish, top with the soured cream and parsley and serve at once. Alternatively, serve on a bed of red cabbage.

SERVES FOUR TO SIX

ℳRS BEETON'S WINTER SALAD

Adding milk to oil and vinegar dressing gives an unusual, slightly creamy mixture. The milk may be omitted, or mayonnaise thinned with single cream; yogurt or milk may be used instead.

1 head of endive, washed and shredded
1 punnet of mustard and cress
2 celery sticks, thinly sliced
4 hard-boiled eggs, sliced
225 g/8 oz cooked beetroot, sliced

DRESSING
5 ml/1 tsp French mustard
5 ml/1 tsp caster sugar
30 ml/2 tbsp salad oil
30 ml/2 tbsp milk
30 ml/2 tbsp cider vinegar
salt
cayenne

Arrange the endive, mustard and cress and celery in a salad bowl. Top with the eggs and beetroot, overlapping the slices or interleaving them with the endive but keeping them separate from each other.

For the dressing, put the mustard and sugar in a small bowl. Gradually add the oil, whisking all the time. Add the milk very slowly, whisking vigorously to prevent the mixture curdling. Continue adding the vinegar in the same way - if the ingredients are added too quickly the dressing will curdle. Add salt and a hint of cayenne. Spoon this dressing over the salad just before serving.

SERVES SIX

𝒲ALDORF SALAD

4 sharp red dessert apples
2 celery sticks, thinly sliced
25 g/1 oz chopped or broken walnuts
75 ml/5 tbsp mayonnaise
30 ml/ 2 tbsp lemon juice
pinch of salt
lettuce leaves (optional)

Core the apples, but do not peel them. Cut them into dice. Put them in a bowl with the celery and walnuts. Mix the mayonnaise with the lemon juice. Add salt to taste and fold into the apple mixture. Chill. Serve on a bed of lettuce leaves, if liked.

SERVES FOUR

VARIATION
Waldorf Salad with Chicken Make as above, but use only 2 apples. Add 350 g/12 oz diced cold cooked chicken. For extra flavour and colour, add small seedless green grapes.

MRS BEETON'S TIP
Pastry fleurons are a useful garnish for salads and cold platters as well as for soups and hot vegetable dishes. Roll out 215g/7oz puff pastry on a floured board.Cut into rounds, using a 5 cm/2 inch cutter. Move the cutter halfway across each round and cut in half again,making a half moon and an almond shape. Arrange the half moons on a baking sheet, brush with beaten egg and bake in a preheated 200 C/400 F/gas 6 oven for 8-10 minutes. The almond shapes may either be baked as biscuits or re-rolled and cut to make more fleurons.

Savoy Cake with Ginger Cream

This light sponge may be used as a base for making fruit and cream gâteaux or for trifles. Originally, the ginger cream was set in a mould to be served on its own as a rich dessert. Combined, the cake and cream make an irresistible dessert duo.

6 eggs, separated
15 ml/1 tbsp orange flower water or rose water
grated rind of 1 lemon
175 g/6 oz caster sugar
175 g/6 oz plain flour

GINGER CREAM
15 ml/1 tbsp gelatine
4 egg yolks
600 ml/1 pint double cream
75 g/3 oz preserved stem ginger, finely sliced
15 ml/1 tbsp syrup from preserved ginger
icing sugar for dredging

Set the oven at 180°C/350°F/gas 4. Grease and flour a 20 cm/8 inch round deep cake tin.

Cream the egg yolks with the orange flower water or rose water, lemon rind and sugar until pale and thick. In a clean, grease-free bowl, whisk the egg whites until stiff, then fold them into the yolks.

Sift the flour over the mixture and fold it in gently. Turn the mixture into the prepared tin and bake for about 45 minutes, until the cake is risen, browned and firm. Turn the cake out on to a wire rack to cool.

To make the ginger cream, sprinkle the gelatine over 30 ml/2 tbsp cold water in a heatproof basin and set aside for 15 minutes, until spongy. Place over a saucepan of hot water and stir until the gelatine has dissolved completely.

Beat the yolks in a heatproof bowl. Stir in the cream, ginger and syrup. Place over a saucepan of hot water and stir until the mixture has thickened sufficiently to thinly coat the back of a spoon.

Stir a little of the cream into the gelatine, then pour it into the main batch of mixture and stir well. Leave to cool, stirring often. Chill well.

To serve, dredge the top of the cake thickly with icing sugar. Serve each slice of cake topped with a generous spoonful of ginger cream; offer the remaining ginger cream separately.

SERVES TEN

Oranges in Caramel Sauce

This recipe should be in every busy cook's repertoire, as it freezes well and can be frozen for up to 12 months. Cool the oranges quickly in the sauce, place in a rigid container, cover and freeze. Remember to allow a little headspace in the top of the container, as the syrup will expand upon freezing. Thaw, covered, in the refrigerator for about 6 hours.

6 oranges
200 g/7 oz sugar
50-125 ml/2-4 fl oz chilled orange juice

Using a vegetable peeler, remove the rind from 1 orange, taking care not to include any of the bitter pith. Cut the rind into strips with a sharp knife. Bring a small saucepan of water to the boil, add the orange strips and cook for 1 minute, then drain and set aside on absorbent kitchen paper.

Carefully peel the remaining oranges, leaving them whole. Remove the pith from all the oranges and place the fruit in a heatproof bowl.

Put the sugar in a saucepan with 125 ml/4 fl oz water. Heat gently, stirring until the sugar has dissolved, then bring to the boil and boil rapidly, without stirring, until the syrup turns a golden caramel colour. Remove from the heat and carefully add the orange juice. Replace over the heat and stir until just blended, then add the reserved orange rind.

Pour the caramel sauce over the oranges and chill for at least 3 hours before serving.

SERVES SIX

*Christmas is not complete
without Mrs Beeton's
Trifle (page 93)*

BLANQUETTE OF TURKEY

bones from a cooked turkey
1 onion, sliced
1 blade of mace
salt and pepper
40 g/1½ oz butter
40 g/1½ oz plain flour
450 g/1 lb cooked turkey, diced
pinch of nutmeg
30 ml/2 tbsp single cream or top-of-the-milk
1 egg yolk

Combine the turkey bones, onion and mace in a saucepan. Add enough water to cover, with a good sprinkling of salt and pepper. Bring to the boil, lower the heat and cover the pan. Simmer for 1½ hours, or longer, to obtain well-flavoured stock. Strain the stock into a jug, setting aside 400 ml/14 fl oz.

Melt the butter in a saucepan, stir in the flour and cook for 1 minute without browning. Gradually stir in the measured stock. Bring to the boil, stirring constantly, and cook for 10 minutes. Stir in the turkey and nutmeg.

Heat the turkey in the sauce over gentle heat for about 20 minutes. Mix the cream or milk and egg yolk in a small bowl. Stir in a little of the hot sauce and mix well. Add the contents of the bowl to the saucepan and heat gently; do not boil. Taste for seasoning and serve at once, with boiled rice or noodles.

SERVES FOUR

VARIATION

Turkey with Cashew Nuts and Bacon Add 100 g/4 oz cashew nuts and 2 crumbled grilled bacon rashers to the blanquette just before serving. Sprinkle with chopped parsley or lightly sautéed leeks.

MRS BEETON'S BAKED VEAL OR HAM LOAF

Leftover roast veal would have been commonplace in Mrs Beeton's day but the recipe will work equally well if cooked ham or other cold cooked meat or poultry is used.

fat for greasing
200 g/7 oz cold roast veal or cooked ham
4 rindless streaky bacon rashers
175 g/6 oz fresh white breadcrumbs
250 ml/8 fl oz veal or chicken stock
2.5 ml/½ tsp grated lemon rind
2.5 ml/½ tsp ground mace
1.25 ml/¼ tsp cayenne pepper
30 ml/2 tbsp chopped parsley
salt
2 eggs, lightly beaten

Thoroughly grease a 450 g/1 lb loaf tin or 750 ml/1¼ pint ovenproof dish. Set the oven at 160°C/325°F/gas 3. Mince the veal or ham and bacon together finely or process in a food processor. Scrape into a bowl and add the breadcrumbs, stock and lemon rind, mace, cayenne and parsley with salt to taste. Mix in the eggs.

Spoon the mixture into the prepared tin or dish and bake for 1 hour, or until the mixture is firm and lightly browned. Serve hot, with gravy or tomato sauce, if liked.

SERVES THREE TO FOUR

MRS BEETON'S TIP
If the loaf tin has a tendency to stick, line the base with baking parchment or greaseproof paper so that the loaf will turn out easily.

HASHED TURKEY

bones from a cooked turkey
1 carrot, sliced
1 turnip, diced
1 blade of mace
1 bouquet garni
salt and pepper
30 g/1 oz butter
1 onion, chopped
40 g/1½ oz plain flour
30 ml/2 tbsp mushroom ketchup or 10 ml/2 tsp Cherokee
Sauce (page 25)
45 ml/3 tbsp port or sherry
6 generous slices of cooked turkey breast

Combine the turkey bones, carrot, turnip, mace and bouquet garni in a saucepan. Add enough water to cover, with a good sprinkling of salt and pepper. Bring to the boil, lower the heat and cover the pan. Simmer for 1½ hours. Strain the stock into a jug, setting aside 600 ml/1 pint.

Melt the butter in a clean saucepan, add the onion and fry over gentle heat for 10 minutes. Stir in the flour and cook for 2 minutes. Gradually add the measured stock, stirring until the sauce boils and thickens. Stir in the mushroom ketchup or Cherokee Sauce with the port or sherry. Add salt and pepper to taste.

Add the turkey to the sauce and heat through for 15 minutes. Serve hot.

SERVES SIX

MRS BEETON'S TIP
Leftover stuffing makes a tasty addition to the hash. Cut it into neat portions and add to the sauce with the sliced turkey.

TURKEY CROQUETTES

This is a simple solution to the problem of what to do with small uneven pieces of leftover turkey, and is suitable for both light and dark meat. Mrs Beeton suggested shaping the mixture into small mounds by pressing it into a small greased wine glass before coating.

15 ml/1 tbsp butter
1 small onion, finely chopped
30 ml/2 tbsp plain flour
300 ml/½ pint turkey gravy or stock
450 g/1 lb cooked turkey, minced or finely chopped
100 g/4 oz cooked ham, minced or finely chopped
2 egg yolks
salt and pepper
flour, egg and breadcrumbs for coating
oil for deep frying

Melt the butter in a saucepan, add the onion and fry over gentle heat until tender. Stir in the flour and cook for 1-2 minutes. Add the turkey gravy or stock, stirring until the mixture boils and thickens.

Off the heat, add the minced turkey, ham and egg yolks, with plenty of salt and pepper. Mix well. Cool, then chill.

Shape the mixture into 6 croquettes. Coat in flour, egg and breadcrumbs, then deep fry until golden. Drain on absorbent kitchen paper. Serve hot, with a mushroom, onion or tomato sauce.

MAKES SIX

New Year Celebrations

WASSAILING

Hard on the heels of the Christmas festivities comes Hogmanay or New Year's Eve. It's a time for rejoicing and reflection, for looking back at the successes (and failures) of the past year and for looking forward to the year ahead; for resolutions and revelry.

Wassailing, which is sometimes wrongly confused with carol singing, is an ancient custom especially associated with New Year. The word comes from the Anglo-Saxon Waes-Hail, a toast which means 'Be whole', to which the reply was Drink-Hail, or 'Good Health!'

In some parts of Britain, villagers and townspeople celebrated New Year with wassailing processions, when the wassail bowl, containing hot spiced ale and sliced or whole apples, was decorated with greenery and carried from house to house. The inhabitants were invited to drink from the bowl, to ensure good luck for the year ahead, and then to refill it. A recipe for hot spiced Mulled Ale is given on page 32.

A Scottish version of the wassail bowl, the het pint, was carried through the streets several hours before midnight on Hogmanay, in large copper kettles known as toddy kettles.

Children sometimes went wassailing to collect fruit - especially apples - and money. The words of one traditional wassail song were quite explicit:

'Wassail, wassail through the town,
If you've got any apples,
throw them down;
If you've got no apples,
money will do,
If you've got no money,
God bless you.'

HOGMANAY FARE

Haggis is *the* food with which to celebrate Hogmanay in Scotland. It is usually served with clapshot (mashed potatoes and turnips mixed with herbs); more familiarly known as 'neeps and tatties'. Haggis (the name is thought to derive from the French hachis meaning 'chopped') is made of chopped offal, oatmeal and suet packed inside the bag of a lamb's stomach and cooked slowly in water. It is always eaten to the accompaniment of the skirl of bagpipes and washed down with neat whisky. This tradition is perhaps most warmly observed on Burns' Night, a celebration in honour of the poet Robert Burns, whose poem 'Auld Lang Syne' provides the words for the song traditionally sung at the stroke of midnight on New Year's Eve.

The traditional Scots Black Bun (see page 16) has taken a step back in time, and is now served at Hogmanay instead of on Twelfth Night.

FIRST FOOTING

The tradition of first footing on New Year's Eve goes back a long way in both England (where it has now almost lapsed) and Scotland, where it is still an important part of the Hogmanay ritual.

The responsibility for whether a household will or will not be blessed with good luck in the coming year rests on the shoulders of the first person to cross the threshold after midnight has struck.

It is generally believed that good luck will attend the house if the first footer is a dark-haired man, bringing with him the traditional gifts of a piece of bread, a lump of coal and some salt. His reward, of course, is a wee dram of whisky.

If the first guest to cross the threshold is a woman or a fair-haired man, the omens are not so favourable.

A corner of the New Year's Eve Buffet: Leek Tart (page 106), Devilled Chicken (page 106), Cheese Eclairs (page 105) and Mrs Beeton's Charlotte Russe (page 108)

GOOD LUCK OMENS

New Year's Eve is all about trying to ensure good luck for the coming year, and finding out what it holds in store.

People used to sprinkle their homes inside and out with water freshly drawn from the well, in a combined act of symbolic cleansing and good luck. In Spain, at midnight on New Year's Eve, people eat twelve grapes, one for each stroke of the clock ringing in the New Year.

In parts of Africa, the new year is greeted with a great deal of noise. Saucepans are banged, lids chimed together like cymbals and car hooters sounded to scare away any evil spirits. In the Channel Islands a figure of old Father Time is buried in the sand with due ceremony. This done, the people are ready to greet the New Year.

In Britain, people used to try to discover their fate in the coming twelve months by all kinds of means. One was to drop molten lead into cold water, and then try to analyze the shape it formed as it set and hardened.

Throughout Europe it is considered bad luck to let a fire go out on New Year's Eve.

PARTY TIME

New Year's Eve is often the excuse for the biggest and most boisterous party of the season. 'Eat, drink and be merry' seems to be the byword. Others prefer to celebrate at home, perhaps with a few friends whom they failed to see at Christmas. A New Year's Eve buffet party, with hot dishes as a change from the cold meats, salads and pickles that inevitably follow Christmas, is the perfect way to ring out the old year and ring in the new.

OUT OF STEP

Not everyone in the British Isles celebrates New Year's Eve on the same day. It depends which calendar you go by.

In the Scottish fishing port of Burghead they still adhere to the old calendar, the one used throughout the country until 1752, which means that the annual festival falls on January 11.

Two ancient local families construct a fire basket, which in Gaelic is known as a clavie, from whisky casks or barrels. This is borne around the town by runners, while onlookers scrabble for the falling pieces of charred wood, which are thought to bring luck for the new year.

New Year's Eve Buffet

Anchovy Toast

1 (50 g/2 oz) can anchovy fillets
100 g/4 oz butter
cayenne pepper
125-2.5 ml/¼ - ½ tsp prepared mustard
6-8 slices of toast

Pound the anchovies and their oil to a paste, then mix with the butter, adding a little cayenne and mustard. Spread on hot toast, cut into pieces and serve.

SERVES FOUR TO SIX

Cheese Eclairs

ILLUSTRATED ON PAGE 103

CHOUX PASTRY
100 g/4 oz plain flour
50 g/2 oz butter or margarine
2 whole eggs plus 1 yolk
salt and pepper · pinch of cayenne pepper

FILLING
25 g/1 oz butter
25 g/1 oz plain flour
300 ml/½ pint milk
75-100 g/3-4 oz Cheddar cheese, grated
pinch of mustard powder

Lightly grease a baking sheet. Set the oven at 220°C/425°F/gas 7. To make the pastry, sift the flour on to a sheet of greaseproof paper. Put 250 ml/8 fl oz water in a saucepan and add the butter or margarine with the salt. Heat gently until the fat melts.

When the fat has melted, bring the liquid rapidly to the boil and add all the flour at once. Immediately remove the pan from the heat and stir the flour into the liquid to make a smooth paste which leaves the sides of the pan clean. Set aside to cool slightly. Add the egg yolk and beat well. Add the whole eggs, one at a time, beating well after each addition. Add salt, pepper and cayenne with the final egg. Continue beating until the paste is very glossy.

Put the pastry into a piping bag fitted with a 1 cm/½ inch nozzle and pipe it in 5 cm/2 inch lengths on the prepared baking sheet. Cut off each length with a knife or scissors dipped in hot water.

Bake for 10 minutes, then lower the oven temperature to 180°C/350°F/gas 4 and bake for 20 minutes, or until risen and browned. Split the eclairs open and cool on a wire rack.

Meanwhile, to make the filling, melt the butter in a saucepan. Stir in the flour and cook over low heat for 2-3 minutes, without colouring. Over very low heat, gradually add the milk, stirring constantly. Bring to the boil, stirring, and simmer for 1-2 minutes until smooth and thickened. Stir in the cheese, mustard and salt and pepper to taste. Cool the eclairs on a wire rack. Fill with the cheese sauce.

MAKES 20-24

VARIATIONS

Ham and Egg Eclairs Omit the cheese. Add 2 chopped hard-boiled eggs, 15 ml/1 tbsp chopped tarragon and 75 g/3 oz diced cooked ham to the sauce for the filling.
Smoked Salmon Eclairs Omit the cheese. Add 75 g/3 oz roughly chopped smoked salmon and 2.5 ml/ ½ tsp grated lemon rind to the sauce for the filling. Smoked salmon offcuts are ideal: up to 100 g/4 oz may be added, depending on flavour and the saltiness of the salmon.
Turkey Eclairs Omit the cheese. Add 100 g/4 oz diced cooked turkey and 30 ml/2 tbsp chopped parsley to the sauce.

ℒEEK TART

ILLUSTRATED ON PAGE 103

8 small leeks, trimmed and washed
2 eggs
salt and pepper
grated nutmeg
25 g/1 oz Gruyère cheese, grated

SHORT CRUST PASTRY
100 g/4 oz plain flour
1.25 ml/¼ tsp salt
50 g/2 oz margarine (or half butter, half lard)
flour for rolling out

SAUCE
15 g/½ oz butter
15 g/½ oz plain flour
150 ml/¼ pint milk or milk and leek cooking liquid

Set the oven at 200°C/400°F/gas 6. Make the pastry, following the instructions given in Mrs Beeton's Apple Flan (page 56).

Roll out the pastry on a lightly floured surface and use to line an 18 cm/7 inch flan tin or ring placed on a baking sheet. Line the pastry with greaseproof paper and fill with baking beans. Bake 'blind' for 20 minutes, then remove the paper and beans. Return to the oven for 5 minutes, then leave to cool. Reduce the oven temperature to 190°C/375°F/gas 5.

Using the white parts of the leeks only, tie them into two bundles with string. Bring a saucepan of salted water to the boil, add the leeks and simmer gently for 10 minutes. Drain, then squeeze as dry as possible. Cut the leeks into thick slices.

To make the sauce, melt the butter in a saucepan. Stir in the flour and cook over low heat for 2-3 minutes, without colouring. Gradually add the liquid, stirring constantly until the sauce boils and thickens. Lower the heat and simmer the sauce for 1-2 minutes.

Beat the eggs into the white sauce. Then add salt, pepper and nutmeg to taste. Stir in half of the Gruyère. Put a layer of sauce in the cooled pastry case, cover with the leeks, then with the remaining sauce. Sprinkle with the remaining Gruyère. Bake for 20 minutes or until golden on top.

SERVES EIGHT

𝒟EVILLED CHICKEN

ILLUSTRATED ON PAGE 103

8 chicken breasts
60 ml/4 tbsp oil
100 g/4 oz butter, softened
30 ml/2 tbsp tomato purée
5 ml/1 tsp mustard powder
few drops of Tabasco sauce
15 ml/1 tsp Worcestershire sauce
lemon or lime wedges to serve

Place the chicken breasts on a rack in a grill pan. Brush generously with oil and grill under moderate heat for 5 minutes on each side.

Meanwhile, prepare the devilled mixture. Beat the butter in a small bowl and gradually work in the tomato purée, mustard powder, Tabasco and Worcestershire sauce. Spread half the mixture over the chicken and grill for 5 minutes more, then turn the breasts over carefully, spread with the remaining mixture and grill for a further 5 minutes or until the chicken is thoroughly cooked. Transfer the chicken to plates or a serving dish and add lemon or lime wedges: the fruit juice may be squeezed over just before the chicken is eaten. Serve with baked jacket potatoes and a salad.

SERVES EIGHT

GRATIN DAUPHINOIS

25 g/1 oz butter
1 kg/2¼ lb potatoes, thinly sliced
1 large onion, about 200 g/7 oz, thinly sliced
200 g/7 oz Gruyère cheese, grated
salt and pepper
grated nutmeg
125 ml/4 fl oz single cream

Butter a 1.5 litre/2¾ pint casserole, reserving the remaining butter. Set the oven at 190°C/375°F/gas 5. Bring a saucepan of water to the boil, add the potatoes and onion, then blanch for 30 seconds. Drain.

Put a layer of potatoes in the bottom of the prepared casserole. Dot with a little of the butter, then sprinkle with some of the onion and cheese, a little salt, pepper and grated nutmeg. Pour over some of the cream. Repeat the layers until all the ingredients have been used, finishing with a layer of cheese. Pour the remaining cream on top.

Cover and bake for 1 hour. Remove from the oven and place under a hot grill for 5 minutes, until the top of the cheese is golden brown and bubbling.

SERVES SIX

RATATOUILLE

ILLUSTRATED ON PAGE 95

Traditionally, the vegetable mixture is cooked gently for about 45-60 minutes and it is richer, and more intensely flavoured if prepared ahead, cooled and thoroughly reheated. This recipe suggests cooking for slightly less time, so that the courgettes and aubergines still retain a bit of bite; the final simmering time may be shortened, if liked, to give a mixture in which the courgettes contribute a slightly crunchy texture.

2 aubergines · salt and pepper
125-150 ml/4-5 fl oz olive oil
2 large onions, finely chopped
2 garlic cloves, crushed
2 peppers, seeded and cut into thin strips
30 ml/2 tbsp chopped fresh marjoram or 10 ml/2 tsp dried
450 g/1 lb tomatoes, peeled and chopped
4 courgettes, thinly sliced
30 ml/2 tbsp finely chopped parsley or mint

Cut the ends off the aubergines and cut them into cubes. Put the cubes in a colander and sprinkle generously with salt. Set aside for 30 minutes, then rinse, drain and pat dry on kitchen paper.

Heat some of the oil in a large saucepan or flameproof casserole, add some of the aubergine cubes and cook over moderate heat, stirring frequently, for 10 minutes. Using a slotted spoon, transfer the aubergine to a bowl; repeat until all the cubes are cooked, adding more oil as necessary. Add the onions to the oil remaining in the pan and fry for 5 minutes, until slightly softened. Stir in the garlic, peppers and marjoram, with salt and pepper to taste. Cook, stirring occasionally for 15-20 minutes, or until the onions are thoroughly softened.

Stir the tomatoes and courgettes into the vegetable mixture. Replace the aubergines, heat until bubbling, then cover and simmer for a further 15-20 minutes, stirring occasionally. Serve hot, sprinkled with parsley, or cold, sprinkled with mint.

SERVES SIX

Mrs Beeton's Charlotte Russe

ILLUSTRATED ON PAGE 103

45 ml/3 tbsp icing sugar, sifted
24 sponge fingers
15 ml/1 tbsp gelatine
500 ml/17 fl oz single cream
45 ml/3 tbsp any sweet liqueur
1 (15 cm/6 inch) round sponge cake, 1 cm/½ inch thick

In a small bowl, mix 30 ml/2 tbsp of the icing sugar with a little water to make a thin glacé icing. Cut 4 sponge fingers in half, and dip the rounded ends in the icing. Line a 15 cm/6 inch soufflé dish with the halved fingers, placing them like a star, with the sugared sides uppermost and the iced ends meeting in the centre. Dip one end of each of the remaining biscuits in the icing; use to line the sides of the dish, with the sugared sides outward and the iced ends at the base. Trim the biscuits to the height of the soufflé dish.

Place 45 ml/3 tbsp water in a small heatproof bowl and sprinkle the gelatine on to the liquid. Set aside for 15 minutes until the gelatine is spongy. Stand the bowl over a saucepan of hot water and stir the gelatine until it has dissolved completely.

Combine the cream, liqueur and remaining icing sugar in a bowl. Add the gelatine and whisk until frothy. Stand the mixture in a cool place until it begins to thicken, then pour carefully into the charlotte. Cover the flavoured cream with the sponge cake, making sure it is set enough to support the cake. Chill for 8-12 hours, until firm.

Loosen the biscuits from the sides of the dish with a knife, carefully turn the charlotte out on to a plate and serve.

SERVES SIX

Pavlova

Vary the fruit filling for pavlova. Strawberries, raspberries, redcurrants, kiwi fruit and bananas are all suitable. If fresh fruit is difficult to come by at Christmas time use well drained, good quality canned fruit and add a little glacé fruit.

3 egg whites
150 g/5 oz caster sugar
2.5 ml/½ tsp vinegar
2.5 ml/½ tsp vanilla essence
10 ml/2 tsp cornflour
glacé cherries and angelica to decorate

FILLING
250 ml/8 fl oz double cream
caster sugar (see method)
2 peaches, skinned and sliced

Line a baking sheet with greaseproof paper or non-stick baking parchment. Draw a 20 cm/8 inch circle on the paper and very lightly grease the greaseproof paper, if used. Set the oven at 150°C/300°F/gas 2.

In a large bowl, whisk the egg whites until very stiff. Continue whisking, gradually adding the sugar until the mixture stands in stiff peaks. Beat in the vinegar, vanilla and cornflour.

Spread the meringue over the circle, piling it up at the edges to form a rim, or pipe the circle and rim from a piping bag fitted with a large star nozzle.

Bake for about 1 hour or until the pavlova is crisp on the outside and has the texture of marshmallow inside. It should be pale coffee in colour. Leave to cool, then carefully remove the paper. Put the pavlova on a large serving plate.

Make the filling by whipping the cream in a bowl with caster sugar to taste. Add the sliced peaches and pile into the cold pavlova shell. Decorate with glacé cherries and angelica. Serve as soon as possible.

SERVES FOUR

New Year's Day Meal

Relax over a prepare-ahead family lunch or entertain friends to an informal meal on New Year's Day. This rich dish of stewed venison is deliciously festive without requiring hours of last-minute attention and the potato croquettes can be frozen well in advance ready for reheating in the oven before serving.

Stewed Venison

Originally, Mrs Beeton used mutton fat in her rolled joint of venison but pork fat or belly of pork is both more practical and tasty for today's recipe. The addition of vegetables to the cooking liquid means that water may be used in place of home-made stock. The cooking juices are strained and served without thickening; for a slightly thickened gravy, beat 25 g/1 oz plain flour with 40 g/1½ oz butter, then whisk lumps of this mixture into the simmering sauce and cook for 3 minutes, whisking all the time, before serving.

225 g/8 oz fat belly of pork, rind removed and thinly sliced
300 ml/½ pint port
1.8 kg/4 lb boned shoulder of venison
salt and pepper
5 ml/1 tsp ground allspice
1 large onion, sliced
1 large carrot, sliced
2 celery sticks, sliced
1 bay leaf
2 parsley sprigs
1 thyme sprig
2.5 ml/½ tsp whole allspice
2.5 ml/½ tsp whole black peppercorns
redcurrant jelly to serve

Lay the belly of pork in a dish and pour the port over. Cover and set aside for 2-3 hours. Lay the venison on a sheet of non-stick baking parchment, cover it with a second sheet of parchment and beat it with a rolling pin to flatten the joint and thin it slightly.

Drain the pork, reserving the port, then lay the slices on top of the venison. Sprinkle with salt and pepper and the ground allspice. Then roll the meat and tie it securely into a neat shape. Lay the onion, carrot, celery, bay leaf, parsley and thyme in a flame-proof casserole. Place the rolled joint on top of the vegetables. Add the reserved port, the whole allspice and peppercorns and 900 ml/1½ pints water. Bring the liquid just to the boil, then lower the heat so that it simmers very gently. Cover the pan tightly. Simmer the venison for about 4 hours, topping up the water as required and basting the joint occasionally, until the joint is tender.

Transfer the venison to a serving dish and strain the cooking juices into a saucepan. Bring them to the boil and boil hard until reduced by about a quarter to make a thin, flavoursome gravy. Taste for seasoning before serving with the carved venison. Offer redcurrant jelly with the venison.

SERVES EIGHT TO TEN

Cauliflower Polonaise

1 large cauliflower, trimmed
salt
50 g/2 oz butter
50 g/2 oz fresh white breadcrumbs
2 hard-boiled eggs
15 ml/1 tbsp chopped parsley

Put the cauliflower, stem down, in a saucepan. Pour over boiling water, add salt to taste and cook for 10-15 minutes or until the stalk is just tender. Drain the cauliflower thoroughly in a colander. Meanwhile, melt the butter in a frying pan, add the breadcrumbs and fry until crisp and golden. Chop the egg whites finely. Sieve the yolks and mix them with the parsley in a small bowl.

Drain the cauliflower thoroughly and place it on a heated serving dish. Sprinkle first with the breadcrumbs and then with the egg yolk mixture. Arrange the chopped egg white around the edge of the dish. Serve at once.

SERVES FOUR TO SIX

POTATO CROQUETTES

450 g/1 lb potatoes, halved or quartered
25 g/1 oz butter or margarine
2 whole eggs plus 2 egg yolks
salt and pepper
15 ml/1 tbsp chopped parsley
flour for dusting
dried white breadcrumbs for coating
oil for deep frying

Cook the potatoes in boiling water for about 20 minutes until tender. Drain thoroughly and rub through a sieve into a mixing bowl. Beat in the butter or margarine with the egg yolks and add salt and pepper to taste. Add the parsley

Spread out the flour for dusting in a shallow bowl. Put the whole eggs in a second bowl and beat them lightly with a fork. Spread the breadcrumbs on a plate or sheet of foil.

Form the potato mixture into balls or cylindrical rolls. Coat them first in flour, then in egg and finally in breadcrumbs. Repeat the operation so that they have a double coating, then place them on a baking sheet and chill for 1 hour to firm the mixture.

Heat the oil for deep frying to 180-190°C/350-375°F or until a cube of bread added to the oil browns in 30 seconds. Fry the potato croquettes, a few at a time, until golden brown. Drain on absorbent kitchen paper and keep the croquettes hot while cooking successive batches.

MAKES TWELVE TO FIFTEEN

BUTTERED LEEKS

50 g/2 oz butter
675 g/1½ lb leeks, trimmed, sliced and washed
15 ml/1 tbsp lemon juice
salt and pepper
30 ml/2 tbsp single cream (optional)

Melt the butter in a heavy-bottomed saucepan. Add the leeks and lemon juice, with salt and pepper to taste. Cover the pan and cook the leeks over very gentle heat for about 30 minutes or until very tender. Shake the pan from time to time to prevent the leeks from sticking to the base. Serve in the cooking liquid. Stir in the cream when serving, if liked.

SERVES FOUR TO SIX

MRS BEETON'S TIP
Leeks can be very gritty. The easiest way to wash them is to trim them lengthways to the centre, and hold them open under cold running water to flush out the grit.

INDIAN TRIFLE

The original idea was to set the rice mixture in a dish, then cut out a star shape from the middle and fill the space with custard. This simpler version is equally decorative and avoids having leftover rice.

45 ml/3 tbsp rice flour
600 ml/1 pint milk
grated rind of 1 lemon
50 g/2 oz sugar
25 g/1 oz blanched almonds
about 50 g/2 oz candied peel and crystallized fruit, roughly chopped

CUSTARD
25 g/1 oz cornflour
25 g/1 oz caster sugar
4 egg yolks
5 ml/1 tsp vanilla essence
600 ml/1 pint milk

Mix the rice flour to a cream with a little of the milk and the lemon rind. Heat the remaining milk until hot, pour some on to the rice, then return the mixture to the saucepan. Bring to the boil, stirring con-

stantly, then simmer the rice gently for 5 minutes. Stir in the sugar. Cool the rice slightly before pouring it into a glass dish. Cover the surface with dampened greaseproof paper and set aside.

For the custard, blend the cornflour, caster sugar, egg yolks and vanilla to a smooth cream with a little of the milk. Heat the remaining milk until hot. Pour some of the milk on the egg mixture, stirring, then replace the mixture in the saucepan with the rest of the milk. Bring to the boil, stirring constantly, then simmer for 3 minutes.

Pour the custard over the rice. Sprinkle with the almonds, candied peel and fruit and set aside to cool. The fruit and nut topping prevents a skin forming on the custard. Chill before serving.

SERVES SIX TO EIGHT

Sacher Torte

Invented by Franz Sacher, this is one of the most delectable (and calorific) cakes imaginable. Serve it solo, or with whipped cream. The icing owes its gloss to glycerine, which is available from chemists.

butter for greasing
175 g/6 oz butter
175 g/6 oz icing sugar
6 eggs, separated
175 g/6 oz plain chocolate, in squares
2-3 drops of vanilla essence
150 g/5 oz plain flour, sifted
about 125 ml/4 fl oz apricot jam, warmed and sieved, for filling and glazing

ICING
150 g/5 oz plain chocolate, in squares
125 g/4 oz icing sugar, sifted
12.5 ml/2½ tsp glycerine

Line and grease a 20 cm/8 inch loose-bottomed cake tin. Set the oven at 180°C/350°F/gas 4.

In a mixing bowl, beat the butter until creamy. Add 100 g/4 oz of the icing sugar, beating until light and fluffy. Add the egg yolks, one at a time, beating after each addition.

Melt the chocolate with 30 ml/2 tbsp water in a heatproof bowl over hot water. Stir into the cake mixture with the vanilla essence.

In a clean, grease-free bowl, whisk the egg whites to soft peaks. Beat in the remaining icing sugar and continue beating until stiff but not dry. Fold into the chocolate mixture alternately with the sifted flour, adding about 15 ml/1 tbsp of each of a time.

Spoon the mixture into the prepared cake tin and set the tin on a baking sheet. With the back of a spoon, make a slight depression in the centre of the cake to ensure even rising. Bake for 1-1¼ hours or until a skewer inserted in the centre of the cake comes out clean.

Leave the cake in the tin for a few minutes, then turn out on to a wire rack. Cool to room temperature.

Split the cake in half and brush the cut sides with warmed apricot jam. Sandwich the layers together again and glaze the top and sides of the cake with apricot jam. Set aside.

Make the icing. Melt the chocolate with 75 ml/5 tbsp water in a heatproof bowl over hot water. Stir in the icing sugar and whisk in the glycerine, preferably using a balloon whisk.

Pour the icing over the cake, letting it run down the sides. If necessary, use a metal spatula, warmed in hot water, to smooth the surface. Avoid touching the icing too much at this stage, or the gloss will be lost. Serve when the icing has set.

SERVES TWELVE

TWELFTH NIGHT

There used to be more to Twelfth Night than taking down the Christmas decorations, reading through the Christmas cards for the last time, and disposing of the tree. The feast of Epiphany, which falls on the twelfth day after Christmas was celebrated for its religious significance, as the day the Three Kings brought their gifts to the infant Jesus. There are several traditional customs associated with Twelfth Night.

The day brought the long Christmas festival to a close and, as such, was looked upon as the last excuse for a round of merry-making.

In the past, there were both religious processions and revelry. Farmers lit bonfires in the fields and danced, sang and drank around the blaze to drive away evil spirits. Guessing games were a popular pastime, the sillier the better. Revellers might be asked, for example, to guess what was cooking on the rotating spit in the farmhouse kitchen. They would be barred the door until they had guessed correctly. If the object was something obscure, like an old shoe or a tin bucket, they might be destined to spend several more hours around the bonfire.

PRACTICAL JOKES

Twelfth Night was regarded as the ideal time to play practical jokes of all kinds. Court jesters, and Morris men with their hobby horses toured the streets playing tricks on the revelling crowds, and collected money for the next round of drinks.

The feast of Epiphany is still celebrated in many parts of Europe, with family parties, pantomimes and presents for the children. In Spain children fill their shoes with barley and leave them outside on Twelfth Night, hoping that the Three Kings will pass that way. The barley is a gift for the camels, and the children hope the Three Kings will reciprocate by filling their shoes with small presents.

HUNT THE BEAN

The tradition of baking a special cake to celebrate Twelfth Night goes back to the days of the early Christian church and beyond. In the Middle Ages whoever found the bean in his slice of cake became the 'Lord of Misrule' or 'King' for the festivities of Twelfth Night, with the finder of the pea as his 'Queen'.

By the late seventeenth century the custom had been elaborated to include a whole clove concealed in the cake and intended to identify its finder as a 'knave'. The custom of baking a Twelfth night cake (or Twelfth cake, as it is sometimes known) is retained in France, with the *Galette des Rois*, cake of kings.

In London, the cast of the play running at the Theatre Royal, Drury Lane, on Twelfth Night enjoys a link with tradition. As directed by the will of the eighteenth-century actor Robert Baddeley, the cast is served Baddeley cake.

In the apple-growing counties, in Kent and the west of England the ceremony of wassailing in the orchards took place on Twelfth Night to ensure a bountiful harvest in the coming year. The trees were sprinkled with cider from the wassail bowl then (each region had its own tradition) the wassailers would fire shotguns into the trees or whip the trunks. To finish off the ceremony, and the festive season, the wassail bowls were refilled with cider, and the health of the next harvest drunk.

QUITE A STRUGGLE

A tradition that dates back the thirteenth century keeps villagers of Haxey, in Lincolnshire, on their mettle all day long on January 6. In the old days, so the story goes, peasants fought to retrieve a landowner's leather hood which was blown away in a gale, and

were rewarded with parcels of land for their trouble.

The custom continues, as the 'boggins', two rival teams from local pubs, struggle for possession of a symbolic piece of rolled up leather. The victorious team line up for their free drinks at the winning pub.

INDOOR TRICKS

Taking down all the decorations is often looked upon as a tedious task; instead, make this a light-hearted evening to end the Christmas season, bring out the board games or cards for an evening's entertainment. Tricks were a favourite in Mrs Beeton's day and youngsters still delight in catching out friends with simple ideas such as these.

How to Remove a Coin Without Touching It

Place three coins on a table, the one in the middle with tails up, the others heads up. Then say that you will remove the coin from the centre without touching it. Move the left hand coin to the far right and this, of course, means that the tails-up coin has been removed from the centre of the arrangement without being touched.

The Juggler's Joke

Take a walnut in each hand and throw back your arms as far apart as possible. Tell everyone that you will cause both walnuts to come into whichever hand they decide upon without bringing your hands together. The method is simple: place one of the walnuts on the table. Still keeping your arms outstretched far apart, turn your whole body around to pick up the walnut in your other hand. There you have it - both walnuts in one hand without touching hands.

TWELFTH NIGHT CAKE

fat for greasing
150 g/5 oz margarine
75 g/3 oz soft dark sugar
3 eggs
300 g/11 oz plain flour
60 ml/4 tbsp milk
5 ml/1 tsp bicarbonate of soda
30 ml/2 tbsp golden syrup
2.5 ml/½ tsp ground cinnamon
pinch of salt
50 g/2 oz currants
100 g/4 oz sultanas
100 g/4 oz cut mixed peel
1 dried bean
1 large dried whole pea

Line and grease a 15 cm/6 inch round cake tin. Set the oven at 180°C/350°F/gas 4.

In a mixing bowl, cream the margarine and sugar until light and fluffy. Beat in the eggs, one at a time, adding a little flour with each. Warm the milk, add the bicarbonate of soda and stir until dissolved. Add the syrup.

Mix the spices and salt with the remaining flour in a bowl. Add this to the creamed mixture alternately with the flavoured milk. Lightly stir in the dried fruit and peel. Spoon half the cake mixture into the prepared tin, lay the bean and pea in the centre, then cover with the rest of the cake mixture. Bake for about 2 hours. Cool on a wire rack.

MAKES ONE 15 CM/6 INCH CAKE

TRADITIONS, CARDS AND GIFTS

THE CHRISTMAS TREE

There is something very satisfying about bringing home the Christmas tree, prickly and pine scented. After the search for the box of Christmas decorations, and the initial disappointment when the tree lights are tested and found wanting, decking the tree remains one of the pleasures of the season.

The first record of a fir tree being brought indoors related to one which Martin Luther illuminated with candles. There are later references in seventeenth century Germany to fir trees decorated with fruits, nuts, sweets and paper flowers.

It was this custom that Queen Victoria's Consort, Prince Albert, brought to Britain in 1841, when he had a lighted tree set up in Windsor Castle, introducing his family to the joy he remembered from his own German childhood.

CHOOSING A TREE

The traditional Christmas tree is the Norway spruce, a native of the mountainous regions of Scandinavia, which grows throughout northern and central Europe and the eastern United States. It is mid-green in colour, with dense foliage and a conical shape.

Pines and firs are rapidly gaining in popularity, and several varieties are grown specifically for the Christmas tree market. These include the Scots pine, which is native to Great Britain. It has blue-green foliage and soft needles. The more sharply scented Lodgepole pine has fuller foliage, and is paler than the Scots pine. One of the best trees for decorating is the Noble fir. Its rigid well-shaped branches have bright green needles with pale undersides.

All these varieties are available in Britain from centres run by a department of the Forestry Commission. The trees, many of which are supplied with roots, come from managed forests, where for every tree felled, two more are planted. Alternatively, look for a label showing that the tree was grown by a member of the British Christmas Tree Growers' Association.

Imported trees include the glossy Nordman fir, which has a reputation for excellent needle retention. It has thick soft needles and a conical shape.

ROOTED TREES

If you buy a rooted tree, you may be able to replant it in your garden after the festive season is over. The best rooted trees are those that have been carefully dug up without disturbing the earth around the root system; the entire root ball is wrapped in sacking to keep the soil in place. The roots should be kept damp and the tree potted in moist earth as soon as

Fine and decorative papers may be used for wrapping gifts, with ribbons, fresh greenery and dried cones or flowers as trimmings. Gold spray paint transforms plain tissue which is the ideal wrapping paper for gathering around gifts of unusual shapes.

the sacking has been removed. Leave the tree in a cool place such as a garage or shed until it is brought inside to be decorated. Keep the soil moist.

Bare-rooted trees (those with the larger roots attached, but no soil) should have the roots soaked in water before being potted as above. As with all Christmas trees, they should be positioned away from radiators or fires.

It is also possible to buy trees in tubs. They may have been grown that way, or lifted with the root system and replanted. If the latter, check that the tree looks really fresh, as any delay between lifting and planting may adversely affect the tree's survival.

CUT TREES

Trees that are over 1.5 metres (5 foot) tall are usually harvested by being cut down. The best way to care for a cut tree (and limit needle drop) is to stand it in a bucket of water in a cool place as soon as you bring it home. Just before bringing the tree indoors, cut off at least 2.5 cm (1 inch) from the bottom of the trunk to encourage it to draw up water. If possible, pot the tree in a container that allows it to stand in water. Alternatively, wedge the tree in a bucket with pebbles or tightly screwed-up newspaper. Top the container up with water every day. Do *not* pot a cut tree in soil as this restricts water from being taken up by the trunk.

The best way to dispose of a cut tree after Christmas is to take it to a recycling centre that will turn it into garden mulch; many local authorities offer this service.

TIPS FOR CONTAINERS

✳ If the most convenient waterproof container - a bucket or old enamel bread bin for example - is not very attractive, do not resort to covering it with coloured tissue or crêpe paper. Any water spilt when watering a rooted tree could have disastrous consequences for the floor covering or tabletop. The paper dyes are notoriously non-fast.

✳ One way of disguising the container is by standing it in a 'planter's' basket. Charity and ethnic shops sell attractive and inexpensive ones.
✳ Disguise round or rectangular containers by covering them with a strip of flexible split bamboo matting, the kind used for sunblinds. Alternatively, resurrect a beach mat for the purpose.
✳ Bind thick string or cord round and round an unsightly container to give it an interesting but unobtrusive texture. 'Paint' the container with glue first.
✳ Plant a table-top tree in an earthenware flower pot. Do not forget to place a non-porous saucer or dish under it.
✳ Cover the soil on top of a planted tree with pulled-out pieces of cotton wool, for an authentic wintry look.
✳ If, despite your best efforts, the container is not as attractive as you would wish, disguise it behind a pile of mock presents (wrapped boxes for decoration only).

EVERGREEN CONE TREE

A table-top tree to decorate a party table, to stand on a pedestal in a room corner, or on a deep windowsill where it will delight passers-by.

YOU WILL NEED

a suitable container, such as a wide, shallow basket
ballast to steady the container, such as a few clean, dry, smooth stones
a piece of chicken wire with 5 cm/2 inch wide mesh
wire cutters
stout wire or stub wires
cuttings of evergreens, such as holly, ivy, juniper, yew, cypress or silvery artemisia - one species only, or a mixture
trimmings - see suggestions below

Cut the wire netting and wrap it to make a cone shape. Carefully crunch the cone to minimise the

size of the holes, taking care to retain the general shape. The circumference of the finished cone base should be almost the same as that of the container rim. Place the ballast stones in the basket. Stand the wire cone on top and fix the shape to the basket, tying it on with a few short lengths of wire.

Cut the evergreens into short lengths and push them into the wire cone. Turn the container around and work from all sides, making sure to keep a neat shape. Trim off any stray or unruly stems.

Decorate the evergreen tree with wrapped sweets, small dried flower posies, small ribbon bows, small baubles, foil stars, cinnamon quills, or nuts.

Tie a full bow of wide satin ribbon or silver or gold parcel ribbon and fix it with a piece of wire to the front of the basket.

Suggestions for Christmas tree decorations, including edible treats and items made from play-dough, are given on pages 142-143.

Wall Mounted Evergreen Tree

Where to put the tree is a problem that taxes may families. In a small house or flat, there may simply be insufficient floor space, especially when extra guests are expected, and there is the added consideration that floor and table-top trees are vulnerable to the attentions of small children and animals.

The answer may well be the wall-mounted tree. Evergreen branches festooned with baubles, bows and beads are a very pretty way to decorate a plain wall in the hall or sitting room. Do not think of them just as alternative Christmas trees, but as attractive and highly decorative optional extras.

Take stock of the wall area to be decorated by the tree, and judge what size and shape will look best - whether the branches should have a natural upward curve, should sweep gracefully down in a shallow arc or (less likely) should be straight.

With this requirement in mind, select just the branch or branches you need. You may be able to use an offcut from a Christmas tree which has been trimmed to give the tree a more even shape, or find a long, flat branch of yew, juniper or laurel.

More attractive still, if you have access to a garden, gather two or three branches of different species, perhaps a long gnarled shoot pruned from the apple tree, and a couple of evergreens such as yew and shiny ivy, complete with clusters of fruits.

Tie the branches together and fix them to the wall as unobtrusively as possible. Trim the branches with baubles, bonbons, tinsel, strings of beads and so on, and tie a large ribbon bow, bouquet style, around the lower stem.

If the wall tree is hung over a lighted fireplace, be sure to keep the branches and any decorations well away from the fire.

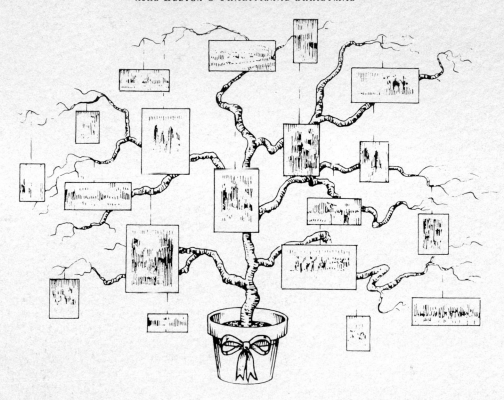

CHRISTMAS CARD TREE

A straggly indoor tree, its frosty-white branches laden with greetings cards, can be a decorative focal point. It is practical too, solving the eternal problem of displaying the Christmas cards where they will not get blown down or knocked over.

YOU WILL NEED

tree stem with many well-spaced side shoots - hazelnut is ideal
spray paint - white, silver or red are most effective
a suitable container, such as an earthenware flower pot or a china or pottery plant holder
soil, quick-setting florist's clay or plaster of Paris, to plant' the tree
a packet of wire tree-bauble hangers
baubles or ribbon bows to trim the tree

Spray the tree branches with your chosen paint. This is a task best undertaken outdoors on a calm day. If it has to be done indoors, cover every surface within nozzle range with newspaper, and spray the branches and shoots a little at a time, from close range. Turn the tree over and spray the reverse side, making sure that it is evenly covered. Leave it to dry.

Plant the tree firmly and securely in the container, using whatever means of fixing you choose.

Decide where the tree is to stand. It makes a difference whether it will be viewed from all angles or (if it is to placed against a wall) just from the front.

Hang the Christmas cards, arranging them to make the tree equally colourful from all sides, or having them all facing forward. Hang the largest ones towards the centre and base of the tree, and the smallest ones at the top and the tips of the shoots.

Friandises (page 138),
Marzipan Fruits (page 138)
and Rum Truffles (page 136).

*E*VERGREENS

An evergreen welcome wreath on the front door, a mistletoe kissing ring in the hall, sprigs of holly over the picture frames, trails of ivy leaves looped above the fireplace - when did the custom of decorating our homes with evergreens begin?

Ancient peoples in many parts of the world believed evergreens to have magical powers, perhaps because their dark and lustrous leaves remained on the branches when all the deciduous trees were bare. They brought evergreen branches indoors to pay homage to their gods, to brighten their homes and rejoice in the natural world during the dark days of winter.

The ancient Scandinavians, in a land of almost constant winter darkness, had a magnificent festival in honour of the god Thor and Mother Night. Evergreen branches and the Yule log were an important part of these celebrations, which marked the beginning of the winter solstice.

The Romans considered evergreens to be a symbol of good luck, and brought them indoors to bestow good fortune on the household for the coming year.

It was not until Victorian times that the practice of decking the home with evergreens reached its peak, and whole families shared in the joy of gathering in the greenery and looping it into garlands to outline stairways, doorways and windows.

There is a special joy still today in 'bringing in the holly'. Anyone who has a garden or the chance to take a walk in the country, taking a trug and secateurs, will enjoy the experience, a rewarding antidote to the rush and crush of Christmas shopping!

Even in the heart of cities, the harshness of winter is softened by the fronds of ivy clinging to walls and colonizing waste ground, and market stalls have bunches of holly and mistletoe to buy.

TRADITIONS AND BELIEFS

Holly In the Middle Ages it was thought that if the first bough of holly brought into the house in winter had prickly leaves, the man would rule the household throughout the coming year. If on the other hand, the holly leaves were smooth and without prickles, the woman would dominate.

Ivy In the Victorian language of flowers, ivy was thought to signify friendship, fidelity and marriage. Like holly, it was considered a symbol of good luck and, if ivy grew up the walls of a house, to protect the occupants from harm and the evil spirits. If this most tenacious and hardy of evergreens withered and died, then that was bad news indeed, and disaster was predicted.

Laurel The fleshy, shiny leaves of laurel have a long association with victory, honour and glory. Laurel branches were among the first to be used to decorate Christian churches at Christmas time.

Mistletoe According to the Victorians, the giving of a sprig of mistletoe signified the overcoming of all obstacles. Its symbolism extends way back to the time of the Druids, and of course sprigs of mistletoe form a traditional part of our Christmas festivities even today.

Pine Bunches of pine were hung indoors in Medieval times to mask the smell of damp and were specially valued in sickrooms for their sweet fresh smell and supposed disinfectant properties.

EVERGREEN IDEAS

* Fill a shallow basket with pine cones and tuck in a few sprigs of evergreens for a lovely contrast of texture and colour.

* Make the most of a few precious fresh flowers, such as lilies or mophead chrysanthemums. Fill a jug with sprays of ivy and high points of twigs, spruce or yew; arrange flowers against this background.

* For a bright and shiny table centre, fill a large glass storage jar with baubles (loopless ones will do). Stick a thin trail of ivy leaves to spiral round the outside, and tuck a thick sprig of ivy into the neck.

* If there really is no space on the Christmas dinner table for a formal decoration it is a charming idea to scatter small sprays of holly or other evergreens on the table among the dishes.

* For a door or wall wreath that looks good enough to eat, wire tiny clementines or russet apples on to a preformed foam ring. Press in evergreen sprays such as ivy, cypress, juniper, to fill in the spaces. For more information on festive wreaths of all types see pages 143-146.

* Hang a shaggy, verdant ball of evergreens in the hall or a room corner. Cut short sprays of greenery and press them into a large potato, which will yield moisture and keep the sprays fresh-looking. Add tiny baubles or ribbon trails for extra glitter.

* Make a buffet table the focus of attention by pinning or tacking trails and loops of ivy to outline the front edge of a cloth. Tiny posies of dried flowers are a naturally pretty extra trim.

* Fill a straw shoulder bag brim-full of evergreens, Chinese lanterns, honesty, spindle berries, whatever, and hang it on the wall.

* Make a decorative version of a carved wooden swag. Ask a greengrocer to save the plaited base of a garlic string, cover it with nuts, dried flowers and evergreens. Wire on the natural materials.

* Traditional evergreen ribbons and swags look marvellous. For step-by-step instructions, see page 144.

MISTLETOE

Throughout the ages mistletoe had been shrouded in mystery. Perhaps this is because it is a parasite, growing on the branches of trees, and was therefore thought to be strange.

The plant played an important part in Druid rituals, a fact that has weighed heavily against it in the eyes of the Christian church, where, in many instances, it is still not allowed to take its place alongside the holly and the ivy in the Christmas decorations.

One exception to this prohibition was York Minster, where a bunch of mistletoe was carried in procession to the high altar as a sign of amnesty to all criminals. The temporary pardon came to an end with the removal of the mistletoe on Twelfth Night.

The Druids gathered their branches of mistletoe in November, ceremoniously cutting it down from the trees with a golden instrument. It was not allowed to touch the ground but was caught on a white sheet.

The mistletoe was divided among the community and clumps or sprigs were hung over doorways to symbolize peace and hospitality, and as a perceived protection against thunder, lightning and evil spirits.

The Druids also used mistletoe as a symbol of fertility, believing it to have magical powers. The plant's innocent association with kissing games at Christmas probably stems from this belief.

In Victorian times, mistletoe was shaped into a ball - to represent the form in which it grows - or bound on to a frame to make a kissing ring. Each time a gallant beau captured a shy maiden beneath the mistletoe and claimed a kiss, the act was recorded by the removal of a berry. When the branch-

TO MAKE A MISTLETOE RING

YOU WILL NEED

one 25 cm/10 inch wire frame, from florist's
a few handfuls of sphagnum or other moss
a roll of medium-gauge binding wire
a selection of evergreens including mistletoe
about 2.5 m/2½ yards satin ribbon, 4 cm/1½ inches wide
about 1 m/1 yard matching satin ribbon, 2.5 cm/1 inch wide

Step 1 Pack the sphagnum moss on both sides of the wire frame and bind it over and over with the wire until it is evenly covered.

Step 2 Cut four lengths of wire about 20 cm/8 inches long. Wrap one round the ring, twist the two ends together close to the ring and shape the remaining length into a loop. Repeat with the other three wires, making hanging loops at equal distances around the frame.

Step 3 Make up bunches of evergreens - holly, ivy, whatever you have - and bind them on to the frame to pack it closely. When the frame is covered, push in the mistletoe sprigs.

Step 4 cut the wide ribbon into five equal lengths. Tie one end of each of four of the ribbons to a wire loop. Bring the other ends together neatly. Staple the ends together, and fix a wire loop for hanging. Cut the narrower ribbon into four equal lengths and tie bows to the loops around the ring.

Step 5 Wire a bunch of mistletoe to the top loop, and tie on a bow.

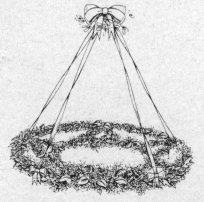

TO MAKE A MISTLETOE BALL

YOU WILL NEED

2 wire coat hangers
wire cutters
a roll of medium-gauge binding wire
about 450 g/1 lb sphagnum or other moss
a selection of evergreens, including mistletoe
about 40 cm/16 inches ribbon, 4 cm/1½ inches wide,
for bow

Step 1 Bend each coathanger to form a circle. Use wire cutters to cut off one of the hooks. Put the two circles together so that the frames cross over, to make the outline of a sphere. Bind the two circles together with wire at the top and bottom.

Step 2 Pack handfuls of the moss around the frame, binding it on with roll wire taken round and round the moss.

Step 3 Compose short sprays of evergreens into small posies, and bind them to the frame, placing them so that the leaves of each bunch cover the stems of the one before. Make sure that the mistletoe sprays are given due prominence. Continue binding on evergreens until the frame is completely covered.

Step 4 Wire a bunch of mistletoe to the base of the ring. Tie a ribbon bow to the top.

*A sophisticated Christmas stocking, made from red brocade and trimmed with lace,
with a selection of home-made crackers. Simple marzipan sweets may be plastic wrapped as stocking
fillers or to place in crackers.*

Christmas Stockings

One of Christmas Eve's particular pleasures, along with setting out a drink and a mince pie for Santa, is the hanging up of the Christmas stockings.

In many households this involves scrabbling around for one of Dad's rugby socks, a carrier bag or even a pillow case. How much better to make a stocking for each child, personalized with his or her name, that can be brought out and hung up year after year?

Why stop at the children? Adults appreciate small presents too, and it is often easier (and less costly) for a child to make and fill a stocking for a parent or grandparent than to buy an elaborate gift.

The idea is worth carrying through to other gift situations too. If a school friend or young neighbour is ill or in hospital, children may contribute a present for a get-well stocking, and if a group of children want to say thank you to a teacher or child minder a gift stocking might prove a perfect choice.

MAKING A STOCKING

The good thing about Christmas stockings is that they come in all shapes and sizes and can be made by people of all skill levels, even those who cannot thread a needle.

If knitting is your forte, take a standard sock pattern, the largest available size, and knit on large needles, using thick wool. Try a progression of colourful stripes, in traditional bright red with white ribbing, in green with a white mock fur trim; whatever takes your fancy.

Cut a Santa from red material, giving him a beard cut from combed white felt or add a Christmas tree shape in looped wool - stockings are fun to make as well as to receive.

If sewing (or even cheating with double sticky tape) is your preference, make up the basic shape from the template and go to town on the decorations. Cut out felt bells, crackers, stars, candles and angels,

embroider the recipient's name in thick yarn, hang tassels of multi-coloured yarns from the top, sew on mini baubles, stick on paper snow-flakes, the choice is limited only by your imagination and skill. Alternatively, of course, you may decide to make a simple stocking in beautiful fabric as a special gift.

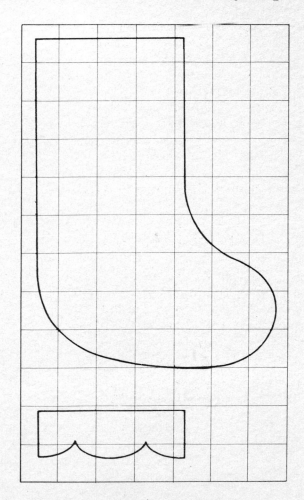

STOCKING FILLERS

Finding the perfect stocking fillers can be quite a challenge, but once you start to think small, it is surprising how much choice there is. The suggestions listed on the page opposite can easily be adapted for all ages and interests.

FOR SONS AND NEPHEWS

Boys and men, people say, are impossible to buy presents for. Pack a stocking with these surprises, and trim it with a bag of gold-foil covered chocolate coins.

puzzle key ring
seed packets if the recipient is a gardener
tin of fruit drops or peppermints
cassette cleaning kit
coloured felt pens
favourite chocolate bars
T-shirt transfer
mulled wine or hot chocolate sachets
golf tees
magazine
voucher for cinema ticket
small pot of Anchovy Relish (page 134)

FOR DEDICATED COOKS

Busy cooks can never have too many of the good things they use in the kitchen. Decorate the top of a stocking with sprays of bay leaves and holly, a cinnamon quill and a couple of heads of garlic.

jars of spices
home-made bouquet garnis
miniature bottles of spirit or liqueur
Hand-Made Chocolates (page 139)
vanilla pods
cinnamon quills
preserve-jar labels
freezer tape
freezer pen
aspic cutters
neck-chain pinger-timer

FOR DAUGHTERS AND AUNTS

Glamorous presents are the obvious choice, but try to include some more intellectual gifts too: a magazine dealing with a specialist subject, perhaps or an offer to fund (fully or in part) a trip to the theatre or ballet. Trim the stocking with a floppy silk flower.

guest soaps
travel-size toiletries
lamp-bulb ring and essential flower oil
token for an hour's ironing/cleaning
pot pourri
fun or glamour tights
fun ceramic brooch
special tree decoration
magazine
butterfly-shape hair clip
earrings
orange cloved pomander
small tin of Rum Truffles (page 136)

FOR FLOWER ARRANGERS

a spray of evergreens and dried flowers to
trim the stocking
florists' adhesive tape
florists' extra-tacky clay
packet of marbles, for stem holding
four-pronged plastic foam holders
floral secateurs
roll of fine or medium-gauge wire
can of gold or silver spray paint
packets of cut-flower feed crystals
flower drying desiccant such as silica gel crystals
false holly or mistletoe berries
small, slender candles
small fir cones
silk flowers
coloured ribbons
water sprayer

GIFT WRAPPING

An attractively wrapped gift can give almost as much pleasure as the gift itself. It could be a small square box wrapped in silver paper, covered with gold sequin trim and tied around with a gold metallic bow, an intriguing cracker-shape decorated with a holly berry spray or a cardboard cone speckled with cut-out paper snowflakes. There are numerous variations. One thing is certain, however modest the gift, if it is wrapped with care and style, the recipient's appreciation will be increased.

Whether your gift is a pearl necklace or a pair of gardening gloves, a bottle of the most expensive cologne or a chain-store equivalent, it makes no difference. The wrapping should be as neat and attractive as you can make it.

It takes time to wrap parcels carefully. Trimming them calls for a little more variety in the bits and pieces drawer than a sheet of last year's paper and a roll of sticky tape, so it is a good idea to plan your present wrapping early, building up a stock of suitable materials and trimmings. Children may like to make their own wrapping paper, using potato cuts with designs of fir trees perhaps.

Gift wrapping can involve the whole family, and does not call on any special skills, except perhaps a little patience. Anyone can cover a box neatly with paper or foil. Anyone can tie it around with ribbon and stick, if not tie, a neat and tidy bow.

Experienced hands at the task begin to see the presentation possibilities before they buy the present - that octagonal-shaped candle could go inside a cardboard tube and be disguised as a Christmas cracker. The less nimble-fingered may start, at least, by matching their gifts to boxes of all shapes and sizes.

PLANNING AHEAD

Think ahead about parcel wrapping well in advance, and start saving anything that might be useful. Boxes are high on the list, and it is worth while keeping as many as you can, stored one inside the other to minimise space. Plastic boxes are sold with gold-wrapped chocolates, wooden date boxes (which may need washing and drying), shoeboxes and ones in which small pieces of kitchen equipment were packed will all prove useful and you have the added satisfaction of knowing that you are recycling items that might otherwise be thrown away.

Boxes that loudly proclaim their former contents or dull brown cardboard ones will need to be covered. For instructions, see pages 128-129.

Scraps and off-cuts from hobby materials make attractive and personalized parcel trims. Fabric scraps can replace paper to wrap small parcels - a box covered in red and white check gingham cotton and tied with a red ribbon bow looks as smart as any wrapped in paper. Scraps of ribbon, braid, fringing, lace edging and bias binding can be used for tying or to make fancy bows or flowers, so save them all.

Snippings of dried flowers - side shoots from large arrangements or flowerheads that have separated from their stems - can be gathered into posy trims or stuck on to plain wrappings; so much prettier than any printed label.

TRIMMINGS

Large parcels wrapped in plain paper can take an exuberant trimming. A pleated paper fan is just the thing. A cluster of curled ribbon ends can look very dramatic too.

Tie the gift box around with three strips of shiny parcel ribbon, leaving long ends for the cluster. Hold each ribbon end close to the knot, between your thumb and the back of a scissor blade. Draw the blade sharply up the length of ribbon so that it curls into a ringlet. Repeat with the remaining ribbons.

Full ribbon and long, slender bows are excellent for decorating any shape of box. The bows also make very attractive Christmas tree decorations.

Father Christmas Cake (page 19)
is simple and traditional

COVERING A BOX

YOU WILL NEED

a box with a separate lid
wrapping paper
pencil
ruler
scissors
adhesive

Step 1 Measure the width of the box accurately, and the depth of sides. Add together the width, twice the depth of each side (to allow for covering inside and outside) and add on another 1 cm/½ inch at each side to allow for turning. For example, if the lid measures 10 cm/4 inches across and the sides are 2 cm/¾ inch deep, you will need to allow 20 cm/8 inches width. Measure the length of the box in the same way. Cut the paper accurately following these dimensions.

Step 2 Place the paper, right side down, on the table. Measure from each end of the paper twice the depth of the lid plus overlap, and mark the corners. Place the lid in position, exactly on those marks. Make sure the paper is taut, and there are no creases.

Step 3 Draw a line from the edge of the paper to a point, which represents the fold-over of the inside of the lid and the overlap. Cut along these lines.

Step 4 Fold the paper over neatly to cover the inside of the depth of the lid. Glue the paper in place neatly.

Step 5 Cut off the excess paper at each corner. Pleat each corner neatly. Pull up the ends of the paper to cover the box and turn over the ends so that they exactly match the width of the box. Fold the paper over inside the lid, run your fingers along the crease, and stick the paper in place.

Step 6 Measure and cut the paper for the base of the box in the same way, allowing for about 2.5 cm/1 inch fold-over inside. Cover the box in the same way.

HEXAGONAL BOX

Covering a box of regular shape is one thing. Neatly wrapping hexagonal, cylindrical or irregular-shaped gifts can be much more difficult. Wrap the paper loosely around the box to estimate how much you need. Allow half the depth of the box for the fold-over at each end. Cut out the paper.

Place the paper, right side down, on the table and centre the box on top. Fix a strip of double-sided sticky tape along one edge (a) and seal the join (b).

At one end of the box, fold the paper towards the centre, making neat triangular folds (c). Pull the sections on each side of it (d and e) towards the centre, then those below the last two (f and g). Lastly pull up h and crease it to a triangular shape. Fold over the excess tip of that section and stick it with double-sided tape. Repeat at the other end.

Decorate the box with a ribbon tied around the centre or towards one end and finished in a bow, with strips of contrasting paper wrapped around, or with a full ribbon bow stuck on to each end.

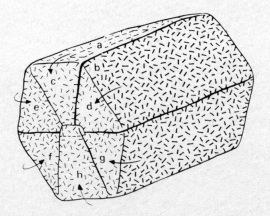

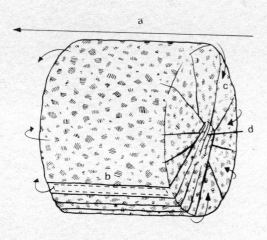

ROUND CONTAINER

Many good things are packed in round boxes and jars, such as special biscuits, preserves and cosmetics. It pays to be adept at wrapping a neat parcel, cylinder style.

Measure the paper by wrapping it around the cylinder. Allow extra width for the pleats. The length of the paper, to allow for a neat finish at each end, should be the height of the box plus just over half the diameter at each side (a).

With the paper right side down, fold over the inside edge and make lengthways pleats along the outside edge. Stick them in place with invisible sticky tape (b).

Stick a strip of double-sided tape along the pleated edge, position the round container, roll the paper around it and seal the overlapping paper edge (b).

To seal one end, fold the paper from the top and down each side in small overlapping sections (c). Lastly fold up the pleated section, turn over the tip and seal with double-sided tape (d).

Repeat at the other end.

Decorate the top with a full ribbon bow.

PLEATED CRACKER

An example of a versatile wrapping that will visually elevate any gift - a pair of socks, a scarf, a jar of sweets, even a seasonal bottle.

Use tissue paper or crêpe paper for the wrapping (this design is pleated) and finish the cracker with a motif all your own, such as a spray of dried flowers.

If the gift is pliable, as socks are, roll it into a sausage shape and wrap it in tissue paper. Cut a piece of card just large enough to wrap around the gift, with a slight overlap at each end (a). Seal the join along the length of the card.

Measure wrapping paper four times the length of the cylinder and wide enough to wrap around it, allowing for pleating. Cut the paper. Fold over one side and pleat the other (b). Enclose the cylinder in the paper and seal the join with double-sided sticky tape.

Grip the paper at each end of the cylinder and tie with ribbon (c). Trim the ends of the paper and tie the ribbon into a bow (d).

Add any festive motif you choose.

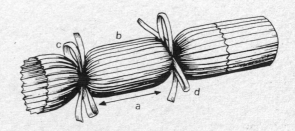

Gift Tags

Children love making their own cards, gift tags and invitations. Settling them down with a pile of old greeting cards, scissors and pinking shears, hole punch and ribbon is a certain way of banishing boredom in the weeks before Christmas - and the results will give a great deal of pleasure.

However, children should not have the monopoly in card design and manufacture. Everyone, whether artistic or not, can make unique examples that convey just that bit more than a bought card.

The most effective gift tags not only convey a brief, bright and cheery message, but also enhance the overall design of the package. Think of the wrapping and the greetings tag as two complementary elements, and design the message accordingly

Off-cuts from a hobby project, such as plain-coloured card in holly-berry red, holly-leaf green or midnight blue may pick out the predominant colour of the wrapping. You could decorate the tags simply with cut-out silver stars, sequins, or white or gold 'snowflakes' cut from paper doilys, or with strips of the wrapping paper - the surest way to achieve a perfect match.

Used Christmas cards can be recycled to yield a variety of different tags. If the front of the card has a particularly attractive design, or a stylized motif such as a Christmas tree, this can be cut out, using plain scissors or pinking shears, in a square, circular or triangular shape. Be sure to check, however that there is no writing on the back of the card.

The backs of used cards may yield enough plain card to cut into single or folded tags. Or you can design tags so that a strip of wrapping paper, Christmas label or other decoration neatly conceals any printing or handwriting.

Add a ribbon loop to each single-thickness tag, or a sticky fixing pad to folded ones, write an appropriate greeting and you will soon have created a selection of highly individual gift tags. It is a good idea to make a variety of sizes too: a tiny card looks lost on a very large box, whereas a tag that is bigger than the present looks silly.

RIBBON TIE

Use a hole punch to make a hole in the corner. Cut a piece of thin parcel ribbon about 30 cm/12 inches long, fold it in half and push the loop through from front to back. Pull the ends through the loop to flatten the knot.

FLAT TAGS

Plain on the back, patterned on the front, a tag may be decorated with a narrow strip of wrapping paper - a row of chirpy robins or frosty Christmas trees for example. Outline the edge of the design with a felt-tip pen if you wish, and stick a strip of narrow ribbon to emphasize the stripe.

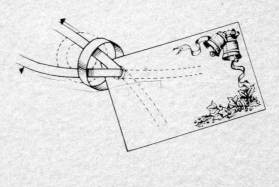

SHADOW SHAPE

A plain-folded card which relies on shape, not pattern, for effect. Draw a pencil line along the right-hand outside edge - a random zig-zag scallop or fluffy cloud effect. Cut along the line then draw around it, on the inside back. Punch a hole in the top left-hand corner of the inside back.

CHRISTMAS CARDS & INVITATIONS

Christmas cards and invitations offer even more scope for design ingenuity and imagination, and making them can become an absorbing hobby in its own right.

You can simplify the task by pasting designs cut from saved greetings cards on to folded white or coloured card, where the shape is suitable, cutting round the outline on one side to give a shadow effect

Or you can design Christmas cards to be pictures in miniature, pressed flower compositions stuck on to the face of a card and protected with cling film. Or make 'window' cards, with an aperture cut from the front to frame a small piece of quilting. You do not need to be an artist with a pen or paintbrush to produce attractive designs.

Children may like to decorate the face of the cards with potato-cut designs, holly leaves and berries, Christmas trees and stars, candles and brightly-coloured flames for example.

If you plan to mass-produce cards for all your friends, and not just make one or two, it is a good idea to buy the envelopes first, and design and cut the cards to fit them. That way, you will achieve the best of both worlds, a hand-made and highly individual card and a professional overall appearance.

SHADOW OUTLINES

Select a wrapping paper or used card motif with a definite, easy-to-cut-out motif (or draw one for yourself). Fold the card in half horizontally to fit the motif and stick it in place. Cut around the shape, leaving a small join at the top to hold the card together. Write your message on the inside back within the outline of the design or on the back.

For a variation on that theme, cut out a simple shape in plain paper - pinking shears give an interesting outline - and stick it to the front of a card folded vertically. Cut out around the outside edge (a). Or cut out and paste only the left-hand half of the shape (b).

Draw the matching outline on the right-hand side and cut it out.

FABRIC COLLAGE

Cut out the card, fold it in half and carefully measure and draw in the 'window' section. Use a craft knife to cut out the window. This piece of card may be used for a gift tag.

Cut a piece of used card - it can be from a cereal packet - slightly larger than the aperture. Cut out strips of fabric to make a design with well-defined outlines. For a landscape scene you could use blue cotton for the sky, green and white cotton for the hill, and felt for the church and moon.

Stick the fabric to the card using multi-purpose glue and leave it to dry. Stick the collage in place in the window of the card and stick a piece of plain paper over the back to cover it.

Christmas Crackers

Christmas crackers have pride of place at party time. The holiday would not be the same without a cracker placed above each setting at the Christmas table, a pile of crackers to make a party go with a noisy swing, and tiny versions decorating the tree. Crackers are surprisingly simple to make from brightly coloured papers and cardboard tubes. Plan colour combinations to match your own decorative themes, trim the crackers in any way you please, and make this a cracking Christmas!

THE ORIGIN OF THE CHRISTMAS CRACKER

Pulling Christmas crackers around the dinner table has, like the Christmas tree, been a part of our celebrations only since Victorian times.

The custom is thought to have derived from France, where children were given bags of sugared almonds on all festive occasions. When pulled in a tug-of-war between rival claimants, or broken open in over-excited handling, the air-filled paper bags burst with a loud bang.

It was a London baker called Thomas Smith who developed the idea and introduced the first proper cracker. Around 1840 he started producing bags of bonbons with an added message, a romantic thought or a riddle, as a sales incentive.

His sales graph did not climb in quite the way he had hoped, and so he introduced an 'exploding strip', a piece of chemically treated card, as an extra novelty.

This certainly had an explosive effect on his business; by the end of the century the Smith company was producing millions of crackers for sale.

By now the crackers also contained 'cosaques'- novelty toys, games, puzzles and hats - and were made in a large range of sizes, colours and designs. The largest cracker Tom Smith produced was said to be 9 metres/30 feet long.

To Make a Cracker

YOU WILL NEED

tissue paper
crêpe paper or crinkle foil in two toning or contrasting colours
cardboard roll - from toilet rolls, kitchen roll etc
double-side adhesive tape
scissors
pinking shears (optional)
paper adhesive
ribbon

AVAILABLE FROM CRACKER COMPONENT FIRMS;

'snaps' in a variety of lengths
small gifts
mottoes
paper hats
trimmings, including gold and silver paper banding and Christmas-design sticky labels

Step 1 Wrap each small gift in tissue paper, to increase the element of surprise.

Step 2 Cut the cardboard roll to length, say 10 cm/4 inches. Push a snap strip through the roll and sticky-tape it in place at one end. Insert the gift, a motto, and a paper hat inside the roll.

Step 3 Measure the decorative paper for the inner layer. Allow three-and-a-half times the length of the cardboard roll (in our example this would be 45 cm/18 inches) and twice the circumference for each cracker. Use pinking shears if you have them to cut the decorative paper.

Step 4 Place the roll in the centre of the paper and wrap the paper firmly around it. Secure the join invisibly, using double-sided sticky tape. This will form the back of the design.

Step 5 Measure the decorative paper in the second colour for the outer layer. Allow twice the length of the cardboard roll (in the example, this would be 20 cm/8 inches long) and the circumference of the roll

plus a small overlap. Cut out the paper, again with pinking shears if possible.

Step 6 Place the cracker in the centre of the paper, right side of the cracker down and the join uppermost. Wrap the paper tightly around the cracker and seal the join with double-sided tape.

Step 7 Gather the paper tightly at each end of the roll and tie it with narrow ribbon. Carefully ease the ribbon knots towards each end of the cardboard roll to improve the shape and cut off the ends.

Step 8 Tie a length of ribbon around each end, to cover the holding knot, and tie it in a generous bow.

Step 9 Insert two or three fingers to open out the cracker ends slightly in order to improve the shape.

Step 10 Decorate the barrel of the cracker in any way you wish. You could wrap a strip of patterned acetate around it to cover a paper name card. This is a good idea, since it enables you to match the gift inside the cracker to the recipient.

DECORATING CRACKERS

If decorative and attractive papers are used to make the cracker, it may not be necessary to add any extra decoration. Plain crackers, however, may be improved by some sort of trim on the barrel. Here are a few suggestions:

* Wrap a strip of gold or silver sequin trim around the centre and sticky-tape it at the back
* wrap around a strip cut from a gold, silver or white paper doily
* stick on flowers or other decorative shapes cut from a paper doily
* stick on a full ribbon bow or a roller bow made from parcel ribbon
* paint the barrel with paper glue and sprinkle on powdered glitter. Shake off the excess powder and, if you wish, stick a doily flower in the centre
* dab spots of glue around the barrel and stick on coloured sequins
* stick on one, two or three dried flower heads. Cornflowers are particularly effective
* stick or tie on a dried flower posy backed by a pressed leaf or small spray of glycerine-preserved leaves of various sizes
* stick or tie on a spray of evergreens; such as yew and holly laden with berries

Food Gifts

Original Scotch Shortbread

Shortbread should be handled as lightly - and as little - as possible; if the dough is worked too much, it will toughen. Wooden moulds, carved with an appropriate motif, such as a thistle, are sometimes used for this Scottish speciality but it is easier to shape the dough by hand.

fat for greasing
225 g/8 oz plain flour
10 ml/2 tsp caraway seeds
50 g/2 oz caster sugar
100 g/4 oz butter, softened
strips of candied peel to decorate

Invert a baking sheet, then grease the surface now uppermost. Set the oven at 180°C/350°F/gas 4.

Mix all the ingredients in a mixing bowl. Rub in the butter until the mixture binds together to a dough. Shape into a large round about 1 cm/½ inch thick. Top the round with strips of candied peel. Pinch up the pastry edges to decorate. Place on the prepared baking sheet, and prick with a fork. Bake for 40-45 minutes. Cut into wedges while still warm.

MAKES EIGHT WEDGES

Potted Cheese

Use a lidded pot when potting cheese as a gift. Add a frilled paper pot cover, made from Christmas wrap.

450 g/1 lb matured Cheddar or Cheshire cheese, finely grated
100 g/4 oz butter, softened
salt
pinch of ground mace
50-75 ml/2-3 fl oz cream sherry or tawny port
melted clarified butter (see Mrs Beeton's Tip, page 65)

Pound about one third of the cheese with the butter

until smooth, or process in a blender or food processor. Add the remaining cheese, with the salt, mace and sherry or port. Pound to a smooth paste.

Turn into small pots. Cover with clarified butter. When cool, refrigerate until the butter is firm.

MAKES ABOUT 450 G/1 LB

Anchovy Relish

Pots of this well-spiced relish make popular gifts, especially with the men of the family. Spread Anchovy Relish thinly on fingers of toast or bread and butter; or use it to flavour canapés. It may also be spread on rounds of toast as a base for serving grilled steak, poached eggs or grilled mushrooms.

1 (50 g/2 oz) can anchovies
2.5 ml/½ tsp allspice
1.25 ml/¼ tsp grated nutmeg
1.25 ml/¼ tsp ground mace
1.25 ml/¼ tsp ground ginger
pinch of ground cloves
2.5 ml/½ tsp Worcestershire sauce
50 g/2 oz butter, softened
freshly ground black pepper

Pound the anchovies to a paste with the oil from the can. Alternatively, process them in a food processor until smooth. Add the spices individually, pounding in each addition, then mix in the Worcestershire sauce.

Add the butter and work it with the spiced anchovies until thoroughly combined. Add pepper to taste. Transfer to a small pot, cover and chill until ready to use. The paste keeps for up to 4 days in the refrigerator.

MAKES ABOUT 75 G/3 OZ

Orange Brandy (page 33), Original Scotch Shortbread and
Anchovy Relish

GANACHE TRUFFLES

Ganache is a rich chocolate cream, made by melting chocolate with cream, then allowing it to set. The chocolate cream may be whipped before it is firm to make a rich topping for cakes; for truffles the mixture is chilled until it is firm enough to be shaped and coated.

350 g/12 oz plain chocolate, in squares
300 ml/½ pint double cream
5 ml/1 tsp vanilla essence
15 ml/1 tbsp icing sugar
cocoa for coating

Place the chocolate squares in a small saucepan. Add the cream and heat gently, stirring often, until the chocolate melts. Remove from the heat and stir in the vanilla and icing sugar, then allow to cool, stirring occasionally.

Chill the mixture until it is firm enough to shape. Place the cocoa in a small basin. Use two teaspoons to shape small balls of mixture and drop them in the cocoa one at a time. Turn the truffles in the cocoa to coat them completely, then place them on a plate or baking sheet and chill again until firm.

MAKES ABOUT 25

RUM TRUFFLES

Packed in plain paper or coloured foil cases and presented in an attractive box covered in appropriate paper (page 128), these would make perfect presents.

50 g/2 oz nibbed almonds
150 g/5 oz plain chocolate, in squares
150 g/5 oz ground almonds
30 ml/2 tbsp double cream
75 g/3 oz caster sugar
15 ml/1 tbsp rum
grated chocolate or chocolate vermicelli for coating

Spread out the almonds on a baking sheet and toast them lightly under a preheated grill. Bring a saucepan of water to the boil.

Put the chocolate in a heatproof bowl that will fit over the pan of water. When the water boils, remove the pan from the heat, set the bowl over the water and leave until the chocolate has melted.

Remove the bowl from the pan and stir in the toasted almonds, ground almonds, cream, sugar and rum. Mix to a stiff paste.

Roll the paste into small balls and toss at once in grated chocolate or chocolate vermicelli. Serve in sweet paper cases.

MAKES ABOUT FIFTEEN

BUTTERED ALMONDS, WALNUTS OR BRAZILS

Brown, buttery and practically irresistible, buttered nuts make a most acceptable gift. Set each one in an individual fluted paper case and pack in a pretty box or tin.

oil for greasing
50 g/2 oz blanched almonds, halved walnuts or whole Brazil nuts
200 g/7 oz demerara sugar
10 ml/2 tsp liquid glucose
pinch of cream of tartar
50 g/2 oz butter

Spread out the nuts on an oiled baking sheet and warm them very gently in a 150°C/300°F/gas 2 oven. Put the sugar into a saucepan, add 90 ml/6 tbsp water and heat gently, stirring, until the sugar has dissolved.

Bring the mixture to the boil. Add the glucose, cream of tartar and butter. When the butter has dissolved, boil the mixture until it registers 140°C/275°F on a sugar thermometer, or test by adding a few drops of the mixture to a bowl of iced water. The mixture should become brittle; a thin piece should snap.

Using a teaspoon, pour a little toffee over each nut; it should set very quickly. When cold, remove all the nuts from the baking sheet, wrap separately in waxed paper, and store in an airtight container.

MAKES ABOUT 50 ALMONDS, 20 WALNUTS OR 15 BRAZILS

*F*RIANDISES

oil for greasing
8 cherries
8 grapes
8 small strawberries
1 satsuma
200 g/7 oz granulated sugar
8 Brazil nuts

Prepare the fruit, leaving the stems on the cherries, grapes and strawberries. Remove any pith from the satsuma segments. Generously grease a large baking sheet and have ready two oiled forks.

Put the sugar in a heavy-bottomed saucepan and add 175 ml/6 fl oz water. Heat gently, stirring until the sugar has dissolved. Increase the heat and boil the syrup until it turns a pale gold in colour. Immediately remove the pan from the heat and dip the bottom of the pan in cold water to prevent the syrup from darkening any further.

Spear a fruit or nut on a fork, dip it in the hot caramel syrup, then allow the excess caramel to drip back into the pan. Use the second fork to ease the fruit or nut on to the baking sheet. Continue until all the fruits and nuts have been glazed, warming the syrup gently if it becomes too thick to use.

When the coating on all the fruits and nuts has hardened, lift them carefully off the baking sheet. Serve in paper sweet cases.

MAKES ABOUT 48

*M*ARZIPAN FRUITS

Marzipan fruits may be packed in paper sweet cases and presented as a charming home-made gift.

White marzipan is better than almond paste for moulding fruits and vegetables because it is smoother and more pliable. It is also more suitable for tinting with food colouring. Study the real fruit, or have it in front of you, to achieve the best result. Use icing sugar to dust your fingers while you work.

Colour one small piece of marzipan yellow and another green as the two basic colours. To do this, knead the food colouring into the marzipan. Small pieces of these colours can be moulded into the remaining marzipan as required. Most fruits are painted for optimum effect; this should be done 24 hours after shaping, when the marzipan has dried slightly.

Use cloves to represent the calyx and stalk on fruit. The fine side of a grater is used to simulate the rough skin of citrus fruits. Mould leaves out of marzipan. The fruit can also be half dipped in chocolate following the technique described for Hand-Made Chocolates on page 139, or rolled in caster sugar. The marzipan can be moulded around a shelled hazelnut or raisin.

Lemon Roll into a ball and ease out to a soft point at each end. Roll lightly on a fine grater.
Apple Roll into a ball, indent top and use a clove for the stalk. Streak with red food colouring.
Pear Gradually taper a ball into shape and put a clove in the narrow end for a stalk. Press another clove well into the rounded end for a calyx. Streak with green food colouring.
Banana Shape into a curved sausage, tapering either end. Colour the tip brown and streak the middle with brown 'ripening' lines using a brown icing pen or food colouring, lightly applied with a brush.
Orange Use orange-coloured marzipan. Mould into a ball and roll on a fine grater.
Strawberry Shape into a ball, then pinch out one end. Paint with red food colouring and sprinkle with caster sugar at once.
Cherries Shape small balls of red marzipan and add long marzipan stalks. These are the ideal shape in which to conceal a hazelnut or raisin.
Peaches Roll into a ball and indent the top, flattening the paste slightly. Brush with a hint of red food colouring.

Note: The techniques outlined above can easily be adapted to make marzipan vegetables.

FONDANT SWEETS

ILLUSTRATED ON PAGE 149

Fondant sweets are made by diluting a basic fondant mix-ture with stock syrup and adding appropriate colourings, flavourings and decorations. A fondant mat is a very useful piece of equipment for sweet making. It consists of a sheet of plastic about 2 cm/¾ inch deep, with fancy shapes inset, into which the liquid fondant, jelly or chocolate is poured. When set, sweets can be removed by bending back the sheet. You will need a sugar thermometer to make fondant.

450 g/1 lb caster or lump sugar
20 ml/4 tsp liquid glucose

STOCK SYRUP
150 g/5 oz granulated sugar

Put the caster sugar or lump sugar in a heavy-bot-tomed saucepan which is absolutely free from grease. Add 150 ml/¼ pint water and heat gently until the sugar has completely dissolved. Stir very occasionally and use a wet pastry brush to wipe away any crystals that form on the sides of the pan. When the sugar has dissolved add the liquid glucose and boil to 115°C/240°F, without stirring. Keep the sides of the pan clean by brushing with the wet brush when nec-essary. If you do not have a sugar thermometer, test by dropping about 2.5 ml/½ tsp of the mixture into iced water. If you can mould the mixture between your fingers to make a soft ball, it is ready. Remove from the heat and allow the bubbles in the mixture to subside.

Pour the mixture slowly into the middle of a wetted marble slab and allow to cool a little. Work the sides to the middle with a sugar scraper or palette knife to make a smaller mass. With a wooden spatula in one hand and the scraper in the other, make a fig-ure of eight with the spatula, keeping the mixture together with the scraper. Work until the whole mass is completely white.

Break off small amounts and knead well, then knead together to form a ball. Wrap in polythene and set aside.

Make the stock syrup. Put the sugar in a saucepan and add 150 ml/¼ pint water. Heat, stirring occasionally, until the sugar has dissolved; boil with-out stirring for 3 minutes. Use a spoon to remove any scum that rises to the surface.

Allow the syrup to cool, then strain into a screw-topped jar, close tightly. Use as indicated below to dilute fondant when making sweets.

MAKES ABOUT 450 G/1 LB FONDANT SWEETS

MRS BEETON'S TIP
Both the Fondant and Stock Syrup may be stored sepa-rately in screw-topped jars until required. Stock syrup should be stored in a cool place (not the refrigerator) and will keep for up to 2 months.

Peppermint Softies Dust a fondant mat with corn-flour. Soften 300 g/11 oz fondant in a bowl over hot water. Do not overheat it. Add a few drops of pepper-mint essence and enough stock syrup to make a cream. Pour into the prepared mat and set overnight.

MAKES ABOUT 300 G/11 OZ

Walnut Fondants Colour 100 g/4 oz fondant pale green and flavour with pineapple essence. Set out 36 walnut halves. Divide the fondant into 18 equal por-tions and roll them into balls. Flatten into pieces about the same diameter as the walnuts. Sandwich one piece of fondant between two walnut halves, pressing firmly. Allow the sweets to harden in a dry, warm place. Serve in paper sweet cases.

MAKES 18

Fondant Fruits or Nuts Any firm fruit that will not discolour may be used. Clean and dry the fruit, removing any stones or pips. Divide oranges or man-darins into segments. To coat 18-20 small fruits or 36-40 nuts, you will need about 200 g/7 oz fondant. Warm the fondant in a bowl over hot water, stirring until it has the appearance of thick cream. Add some stock syrup if necessary. Dip the fruits or nuts indi-

vidually in the fondant and place on a plate to dry. Cherries and grapes can be held by the stem, but other fruits and nuts must be immersed and lifted out with a fork. Use within two days.

HAND-MADE CHOCOLATES

ILLUSTRATED ON PAGE 149

Many sweets are suitable for coating with chocolate. Try Fondant Sweets (opposite), caramels, nougat, coconut ice, flavoured marzipan cut into fancy shapes, small pieces of glacé pineapple or preserved ginger or nuts. The process takes time and patience. Good-quality chocolate with a high cocoa fat content, available from supermarkets or delicatessens, should be used. This is a prepared equivalent of couverture and it may be sold as cooking chocolate or confectioners' chocolate. True couverture chocolate, available from sugarcraft specialists, has nominally more cocoa fat but it has to be tempered before use, a specialist processing of melting and cooling. Alternatively, use a commercial dipping or coating chocolate. The flavour is not so good as that of couverture, but the product is less expensive.

For dipping food the consistency should be thick enough to coat the back of a spoon. You will need a good depth of melted chocolate to dip food successfully; it should be at least 5 cm/2 inches deep.

Line a baking sheet or wire rack with a sheet of waxed paper or non-stick baking parchment. Have ready all the sweets or fillings to be dipped and start with firm items, such as nuts. Spear the sweet on a dipping fork, dip it into the chocolate to the depth required, then quickly withdraw it at the same angle at which it was plunged. Do not rotate part-dipped items in the chocolate or the top line of chocolate will be uneven. Gently shake the food to allow the excess chocolate to fall back into the bowl, then place it on the prepared sheet or rack to dry.

MINI MERINGUES

2 egg whites
pinch of salt
90 g/3½ oz caster sugar, plus extra for dusting
pinch of baking powder (optional)

Line a baking sheet with oiled greaseproof paper or with non-stick baking parchment. Set the oven at 110°C/225°F/gas ¼.

Combine the egg whites and salt in a mixing bowl and whisk until the whites are very stiff and standing in points. They must be completely dry. Gradually add half the caster sugar, 15 ml/1 tbsp at a time, whisking well after each addition until the meringue is stiff. If the sugar is not thoroughly blended in it will form droplets of syrup which may brown, spoiling the appearance and texture of the meringues, and making them difficult to remove from the paper when cooked.

When half the sugar has been whisked in, sprinkle the rest over the surface of the mixture and, using a metal spoon, fold it in very lightly with the baking powder, if used. Put the meringue mixture into a piping bag fitted with a medium nozzle and pipe very small meringues on the paper.

Dust the meringues lightly with caster sugar, then dry off in the oven for 2-3 hours, until they are firm and crisp but still white. If the meringues begin to brown, prop the oven door open a little. When they are crisp on the outside, lift the meringues carefully off the sheet, using a palette knife. Turn them on to their sides and return to the oven until the bases are dry. Cool on a wire rack.

MAKES 24 TO 30 MINI MERINGUES

Iced Petits Fours

fat for greasing
75 g/3 oz plain flour
2.5 ml/½ tsp salt
50 g/2 oz Clarified Butter (see Mrs Beeton's Tip, page 65)
or margarine
3 eggs
75 g/3 oz caster sugar

FILLING
jam or lemon curd

ICING AND DECORATION
100 g/4 oz icing sugar, sifted
food colouring (optional)
crystallized violets
silver balls · glacé fruits
angelica
chopped nuts

Line and grease a 25 x 15 cm/10 x 6 inch rectangular cake tin. Set the oven at 180°C/350°F/gas 4.

Sift the flour and salt into a bowl and put in a warm place. Melt the clarified butter or margarine without letting it get hot. Set aside.

Whisk the eggs lightly in a mixing bowl. Add the sugar and place the bowl over a saucepan of hot water. Whisk for 10-15 minutes until thick. Take care that the bottom of the bowl does not touch the water. Remove from the heat and continue whisking until at blood-heat. The melted butter or margarine should be at the same temperature.

Sift half the flour over the eggs, then pour in half the melted butter or margarine in a thin stream. Fold in gently. Repeat, using the remaining flour and fat. Spoon gently into the prepared tin and bake for 30-40 minutes. Cool on a wire rack.

Cut the cold cake in half horizontally, spread with the chosen filling and sandwich together again. Cut the cake into small rounds, triangles or squares and place on a wire rack set over a large dish. Brush off any loose crumbs.

Place the icing sugar in a bowl. Using a wooden spoon gradually stir in sufficient water (about 15 ml/1 tbsp) to create a glacé icing whose consistency will coat the back of the spoon thinly. Tint part of the icing with food colouring if wished. Using a small spoon, coat the tops and sides of the cakes with the icing or, if preferred, pour it over the cakes, making sure that the sides are coated evenly all over. Decorate the tops of the cakes and leave to set. The cakes may be served in paper cases, if liked.

MAKES 18 TO 24

Brandy Snaps

fat for greasing
50 g/2 oz plain flour
5 ml/1 tsp ground ginger
50 g/2 oz margarine
50 g/2 oz soft dark brown sugar
30 ml/2 tbsp golden syrup
10 ml/2 tsp grated lemon rind
5 ml/1 tsp lemon juice

Grease two or three 25 x 20 cm/10 x 8 inch baking sheets. Also grease the handles of several wooden spoons, standing them upside down in a jar until required. Set the oven at 180°C/350°F/gas 4.

Sift the flour and ginger into a bowl. Melt the margarine in a saucepan. Add the sugar and syrup and warm gently, but do not allow to become hot. Remove from the heat and add the sifted ingredients with the lemon rind and juice. Mix well.

Put spoonfuls of the mixture on to the prepared baking sheets, spacing well apart to allow for spreading. Do not put more than 6 spoonfuls on a baking sheet. Bake for 8-10 minutes.

Remove from the oven and leave to cool for a few seconds until the edges begin to firm. Lift one of the biscuits with a palette knife and roll loosely around the greased handle of one of wooden spoons. Allow to cool before removing the spoon handle. Repeat with the remaining biscuits.

MAKES FOURTEEN TO EIGHTEEN

DECORATIONS

There are many ways to make Christmas a truly sparking occasion. Not least of these are the decorations you choose for your home. Your themes could be all white or traditional holly green and berry red. You could add lavish touches of silver and gold. This is easy and inexpensive to achieve with chain-store baubles, spray-painted twigs and shiny ribbons. Or you could choose a less traditional but equally effective colour theme, such as dark blue and brilliant orange, or purple and gold. There's no need to buy expensive paper chains and garlands: these can easily be made at home.

Decorating the tree can be great fun for all the family, particularly if they have had a hand in making the decorations. Gingerbread Santas and stars are easy to make, look remarkably effective, and can be presented as impromptu gifts to unexpected guests. More durable playdough decorations can be used in a variety of ways: to hang on the tree, to create a nativity scene or for a table centrepiece.

The tradition of decorating the home with evergreens predates the Christmas festival itself. Whether you cut informal armfuls of holly and ivy, or a bunch of mixed greenery just before Christmas, you will find foliage the most versatile and varied decoration of all. Collect as many different evergreens as you can. Those with glistening, shiny leaves will reflect every shaft of candle and firelight, and sprays of matt-surfaced foliage will, by their very contrast, flatter the holly and ivy.

If you give all the boughs of greenery a good, long drink in tepid water as soon as you bring them indoors, they will stay fresh-looking for the twelve days of Christmas and more, even if you arrange them with no source of moisture at all. Candles have a special part to play in the joy and sparkle of Christmas, and can be the inspiration for numerous table decorations.

PAPER CHAINS AND GARLANDS

Making paper chains is an easy, relatively unmessy job that will keep children and adults happily occupied for hours. Provide an assortment of papers (including light card, crêpe paper, foil and tissue), scissors, a stapler and paper glue.

The simplest chain is made by twisting two strips of crêpe paper together. Select two colours, cut a 3.5 cm/1¼ inch strip off the bottom of each folded pack of paper, unfold one end of each strip and staple them together. Twist the strips, unfolding them as you do so. This can be turned into a game, with two children crossing each other the make the twist.

Another simple chain is made by stapling the strips at right angles to each other. Fold each strip across the other in turn, keeping a square shape, until both strips are used up. Fix the ends firmly together with sticky tape, then gently shake out the streamer.

Ring chains are also popular. Cut strips of light card, each about 20 cm/8 inches long and 2 cm/¾ inch wide. Glue or staple a strip together to make a ring, then add a second ring in a contrasting colour, linking it with the first before closing it.

To make a star chain, cut out two six-sided stars from coloured card. Using one star as a template, cut about 50 matching stars from folded tissue paper. Glue the stars together in pairs, using glue only on the top point and alternate points thereafter. When the pairs of stars are dry, glue them together to make the chain, this time using the glue on the points previously uncovered. Finish the chain with a card star at each end for added strength.

Dried Flower Decorations

Dried flowers, with their crisp and crackly petals and bright and shiny looks, make natural looking tree decorations which are especially pretty on green or silver everlasting trees.

* Fill tiny baskets with dried flowerheads in any colours to suit your theme.
* Make tiny posies of mixed flowers and tie them with ribbon bows.
* Thread the zingy orange seedpods of Chinese lanterns on to thick cotton to make bright flower chains.
* Buy the cheapest miniature crackers you can find (or make your own). Stick single strawflower heads or tiny dried flower posies in the centre as a prettier-than-usual motif.
* Spray teasels, those spiky, egg-shaped seed carriers, in your chosen colour and tie each short stem with a ribbon bow.

Edible Tree Decorations

Follow the charming Victorian tradition of decorating the Christmas tree with tempting goodies. They make delightful take-home presents for young visitors, and delectable extra treats for the family.

* Make chains of wrapped sweets to drape from branch to branch. Choose boiled sweets or toffees wrapped in brightly coloured cellophane. Glue the ends of the paper wrappers together.
* Alternatively, tie the sweetie-strings into circles and loop them over the tips of branches.
* Buy a packet of large pretzels, the salty, savoury snacks to enjoy with drinks, an hang them on the tree. The shapes are fascinating and the salt crystals glisten like frost.

* Fill mini baskets with a mixture of nuts and tiny tree baubles - a decorative way to use any that have lost their loops.
* Make gingerbread men, bells, stars, trees, boots, sacks - any shape you can cut with your biscuit cutters or devise yourself. The basic recipe follows. Children love decorating the biscuits with coloured glacé icing, silver confectionery balls and coloured dragées. And they enjoy eating them!

Gingerbread Decorations

225 g/8 oz self-raising flour
2.5 ml/½ tsp salt
5 ml/1 tsp mixed spice
10 ml/2 tsp ground ginger
100 g/4 oz margarine
75 g/3 oz soft light brown sugar
45 ml/3 tbsp milk, plus extra for brushing

Set the oven at 200°C/400°F/gas 6. Grease 2-3 baking sheets. Sift the flour, salt and spices into a mixing bowl. Rub in the margarine until the mixture resembles coarse breadcrumbs. Stir in the sugar and milk and mix to a fairly stiff dough.

Roll out the dough on a lightly-floured board. Cut into decorative shapes. Gather up the trimmings, shape them into a ball, roll out the dough and cut out more biscuits. Place the biscuit shapes on a greased baking sheet and brush them lightly with milk.

Bake in the oven for 15 minutes, or until the biscuits are golden brown. Transfer them to a wire rack and leave them to cool.

Decorate with glacé icing, confectionery balls, candy-coated chocolate drops and hundreds and thousands. When the icing is dry, thread the decorations on ribbon and tie them to the tree.

PLAY-DOUGH DECORATIONS

No matter how frenzied the activity in the kitchen and the household in general, however many cards there are to write and presents to wrap, time can tick by slowly for children impatient for Christmas Day to dawn. Making play-dough shapes is an excellent way of passing the time productively, and will bear decorative fruit for years to come.

The shapes can be as simple as the young designer pleases. A plain ring twisted and baked to a toasty-brown, dangling from a bright red ribbon looks just as enchanting as a complicated plait or a flower with multi-coloured petals. If you wish to make cut-out shapes and do not have suitable biscuit cutters, draw round shapes from Christmas cards or colouring books and make card templates.

Do not allow children to get so carried away with the excitement of the craft that they expect to be able to eat the decorations after all. They are unbearably salty - the mixture is called salt dough in the United States - and in any case they are baked to an unpalatable degree of hardness. They have to be. Any residual moisture would encourage the growth of mould, and the decorations would lose one of their major advantages, that they are virtually everlasting.

THE BASIC DOUGH

450 g/1 lb plain flour
175 g/ 6 oz salt
10 ml/2 tsp glycerine
water (see method)
food colourings (optional)

GLAZE (optional)
1 egg yolk
15 ml/1 tbsp milk

Mix together the flour, salt and glycerine. Pour on enough water to make a fairly stiff dough. Shape the dough into a ball and put it in a plastic bag. Leave it in the refrigerator for several hours, or overnight.

The next day, knead the dough by hand, or in a food processor until smooth. If you want to colour the dough, this is the time to do it. Tear off small pieces of the dough, put them into bowls and sprinkle on one or two drops of food colouring. Knead thoroughly. If the colour is too intense, add more plain dough and knead again.

Roll out the dough on a lightly floured board to an even thickness of about 6 mm/ 3/16 inch. Do not make tree decorations too thick or they will hang heavily on the branches. Cut out the shapes you require, or mould the dough to make fruit, 'mince pies' and so on.

To make plaits, one of the traditional salt-dough decorations, cut three strips about 2 cm/¾ inch wide. Roll the strips to make sausage shapes. Press one end of each of the strips together and plait them in the usual way. Cut off the dough at the ends, shape the plait into a circle and press the joined ends together. Cut out bow or leaf shapes to cover the join, or cover it with a ribbon after baking.

Use a toothpick to press a hole into solid shapes, for the hanging ribbon. Mark on any texture details, such as leaf veins.

Brush uncoloured dough with a glaze of beaten egg and milk and place the shapes well apart on a baking sheet. Leave them in a warm room for at least 24 hours so that they dry thoroughly before baking.

Set the oven at 160°C/325°F/gas 3. Bake the dough for 1-1½ hours or until the shapes are completely dry. Remove them from the oven and leave them to cool.

If you wish, paint the cool dough shapes with clear varnish, to make sure that they catch every sparkle from the tree lights.

Thread ribbon through hanging decorations.

WELCOME WREATHS

The first glimpse guests have of your Christmas decor is when they step up to your front door.

The idea of hanging a welcome wreath of evergreens dates back to Roman times, when a garland of leaves signified good luck and good fortune. The Victorians took up the basic theme and embellished it by adding bonbons and baubles, tokens and treats.

The basic design is infinitely variable, based on a preformed polystyrene foam-filled ring, decorated with holly, ivy, cypress, nuts, cones, dried flowers and ribbon bows. Having made a welcome wreath for the front door you can then carry through the idea as an indoor decoration.

BASIC DOOR WREATH

YOU WILL NEED

a 23 cm/9 inch polystyrene foam-filled ring,
available from florists.
a roll of medium-gauge wire for hanging,
and wiring cones etc
a selection of short sprays of evergreens such as holly,
ivy, juniper, cypress, yew, spruce
a selection of nuts, cones, false berries, miniature baubles,
dried flowers or other trims.
about 60 cm/24 inches of 4 cm/1½ inch wide satin
ribbon for bow

Step 1 Bind the wire round and round the plastic ring and twist the ends into a loop.

Step 2 Select any cones or nuts you want to include in the design. These will need to be twisted on to wires, to make them secure enough for a vertical-hanging design. Cut lengths of wire about 13 cm/5 inches long. To wire cones, press the wire between one layer of 'petals', bring together the two ends and twist them to form a stem. Wrap the wire around each nut and twist the ends.

Wiring cones and nuts

Step 3 Cover the ring generously with short sprays of evergreens of your choice. You can use only holly or a blend of several species.

Step 4 Add to the basic design as you wish, arranging cones, nuts, false holly berries or baubles. Dried flowers are not suitable trimmings for a wreath in a windy or exposed outdoor position.

Step 5 Tie the ribbon into a full bow or a double bow and wire to the top or base of the design. Hang the wreath on a hook on the door, or wire it to the door knocker.

VARIATIONS ON THE THEME

Spruce Ring Use offcuts from the Christmas tree - the shaggy ends that need trimming - to make a spruce ring for a door or fireplace wall. Longer sprays at the top, breaking the neat circular look, make the design unusual and interesting.

Dried Flower Ring For a front door protected by a storm porch, or a design to display inside, the basic wreath can be made very attractive with small posies of dried flowers (wire the stems to make miniature bunches) and seedheads.

A lucky horseshoe

Lucky Horseshoe Make a 'lucky horseshoe' design in the usual way. Cut a one-third segment from the polystyrene ring, using a sharp kitchen knife. (You can use this section to make a crescent-shaped table decoration). Bind a wire round the top of the horse-shoe to form a hanging loop, and fill in the shape with evergreens. Arrange spiky, trailing ends to emphasize the effect.

Evergreen Posy A design with all the freedom you could wish - a shaggy 'posy' of apple twigs, spruce, ivy, laurel and holly. Bind a few cones to the twigs. Bind the stems firmly, and be generous with the ribbon bow.n

A dried flower ring

An evergreen posy

To MAKE A SWAG

YOU WILL NEED

a piece of thick cord
sphagnum or other moss
a roll of medium-gauge wire
a selection of trimmings, such as nuts, cones, small cones,
small fruits, dried flowers and seedheads,
baubles, ribbon bows
ribbon for large decorative bows

Step 1 Measure the cord for the space allocated, allowing for graceful drapes. Cut the cord and, if the garland is to be looped in the centre, mark that point.

Step 2 Pack handfuls of moss round the cord and bind it on, taking the wire round and round.

Step 3 Cut the evergreens into short, even sprays and gather them into bunches.

Step 4 Work from one end towards the centre of the rope. Place the first bunch, stem ends towards the centre, against the end of the rope. Arrange the stems so that the foliage completely covers the front of the rope and bind on the stems. Place the next bunch so that the foliage covers the stems of the first, and bind that in place. Continue until you reach the centre of the rope. Repeat the design on the other side.

Step 5 Bind on more foliage to cover the stem overlap in the centre of the design.

Step 6 Add the chosen decorations. Nuts and cones and small fruits will need to be wired.

Step 7 Hang the garland in place. Tie ribbon bows - perhaps one in the centre and one at each end - and wire them in place.

FINISHING TOUCHES

Silver Balls Wire chestnuts, spray them with silver paint and leave them to dry. Decorate the garland with the nuts, silver baubles, sprays of honesty clusters or white everlasting flowers and silver ribbons.

The Scandinavian Look Make the garland with spiky shoots cut from a Christmas tree. Decorate it with tiny red and white ribbon bows wired to the branches and long trailing bows in matching ribbons at the hanging points.

Fruit and Nut Design Trim the garland with tiny clementines, apples and nuts, including a few pecans if possible, for their unusual and warm colour. Twine thin strands of dried orange peel among the evergreens. For a light-weight alternative, substitute Chinese lanterns for the fruits.

Lazy Ribbon If your fireplace wall is not made to take a hanging decoration, make a garland to rest on the mantelpiece and trail over the ends. Tack care that there is no possibility of the swag's catching fire. A safer idea might be to place the swag along a wide windowsill or on top of a low cupboard or bookcase.

TABLE-TOP WREATHS

*The traditional advent wreath incorporates four candles,
which are lit in sequence as Christmas approaches.
Never leave lighted candles unattended in a room, especially
in a household where there are young children or pets.*

BASIC TABLE-TOP WREATH

YOU WILL NEED

one 23 cm/9 inch polystyrene foam-filled ring, available
from florists
four 23 cm/9 inch non-drip candles
a selection of short sprays of evergreens
a selection of dried flowers, seedheads, nuts, false berries,
miniature baubles or other trims
about 50 cm/20 inches of 2.5 cm/1 inch wide ribbon for
bow
a short length of thin wire

Step 1 Place the ring on a flat surface. Press one candle firmly into the foam, then position the other three at equal distances around the ring.
Step 2 Insert short sprays of evergreens around the ring. Take care that the leaves hang low all over the ring to conceal the casing.

Step 3 Continue to fill in the ring, clustering short leaf sprays around the base of the candles. Turn the ring around to check that it is equally attractive from every angle.
Step 4 Add colourful trimmings, grouping them around the candles, concentrating the visual interest around a single candle - if, for example, the wreath is to be placed on a side table and viewed from one side - or distributing them evenly all-round.

Step 5 Tie the ribbon into a bow and trim the ends. Thread the wire through the back of the loop and twist the ends. Press the wire into the foam to position the bow on the side of the design.

The Christmas Table

Christmas comes but once a year – and so does the Christmas dinner. In most households the festive meal is the most expansive and the most formal one in the annual calender.

It may be the only occasion when the extra leaf is put into the dining table; when all the chairs are put around it, and when every last vegetable dish and sauceboat is in use. If this is to be your first at-home Christmas, or the first one in a new home, it may well be your first opportunity to see how the whole scene comes together.

The occasion is too important, and Christmas Day itself too packed with activity, to leave any detail to chance. Before the houseguests arrive or the last-minute cooking begins, check the arrangements.

Extend the table if necessary and place the chairs around it. Mentally calculate how you will seat your guests. Will there be enough room for everyone at the dining table, or would it be more sensible to seat the children at an adjoining table or create a T-shape by using a trestle table at right angles to the existing table?

Christmas dinner is meant to be a friendly occasion and the table is expected to resemble a 'groaning board', but it should not be so cramped that it looks untidy, nor so overcrowded that guests can scarcely find space to rest a glass in safety.

It may be wise to consider carving the meat at a side table and passing the vegetables around for guests to help themselves from a large serving plate - the way it used to be done.

If placing the cutlery and all the glasses appears likely to pose space problems, consider setting out the dessert spoons and forks, the fruit knives, and the dessert wine and liqueur glasses once the main course has been cleared away.

Having planned the layout of the dining room, it is worth spending a few moments checking the details.

If you plan to use the family silver, does it need polishing? Seldom-used glasses get dusty, so it is a good idea to wash the glassware so that all it requires on Christmas morning is a final polish with a soft cloth.

Is the tablecloth presentable? A crisp white cotton or linen cloth, still the most traditional and most flattering background for food, looks wonderful, but only if it is crisp, and sparkling white. Fold lines can spoil the appearance of a cloth; if you can find time on Christmas day, iron the tablecloth (or hand over the task to that relative who keeps asking what he or she can do to help) just before laying the table.

If you do not have a cloth large enough for the extended table, improvise with a freshly laundered sheet. A lace cloth, placed over a coloured sheet, looks very effective, and it does not matter if it covers the cloth only partially.

PLACING THE CUTLERY

The general rule is that cutlery should be set in the order in which it is to be used, working from the outside inwards, towards the plate. In this way, guests should be able to tell at a glance how many courses are to be served.

Lay the knives, blades pointing inwards, with the spoons on the right side of the plate, and forks on the left. This layout should always be followed, even for a left-handed guest.

To save space from the sides of the place settings an alternative layout is to place the cheese knife on the side plate and the dessert spoon and fork (with handles pointing right and left respectively) above the plate.

PLACING THE WINE GLASSES

Arrange the glasses in a straight line across the top of the right-hand cutlery, in the order of use. This may be a tumbler for water on the right, then a glass for white wine, then one for red wine and lastly a glass for port or liqueur, on the left of the row.

Making Fondant Sweets
(page 157) and Hand-Made
Chocolates (page 159)
is part of the festive fun

FLOWERS FOR THE TABLE

Flowers have a very special role to play on the Christmas dinner table. A somewhat delicate role, since they should provide the pretty finishing touches without at any time detracting by either sight or smell from the food.

Tall containers such as candlesticks, wine carafes converted to elegant table pedestals, and long, narrow specimen-bloom vases are economical with table space. You can compose a cascade of evergreen leaves and berries, a crescent of freesias and spray carnations, or a shower of gypsophila and rosebuds in a container that takes up no more of the table surface than a coffee cup or wine glass. Alternatively, set miniature flower arrangements at each table setting or, if space really is at a premium, place a more elaborate flower arrangement (or a table wreath like the one featured on page 146) on a sideboard or serving table.

If space permits, a three-pronged candle-holder in silver-plate, wrought iron, brass or wood, can easily be converted into a delightful floral centrepiece. Make sure that when it is in place, it does not obstruct any of the guests' view of each other.

ℂENTREPIECE

YOU WILL NEED

a suitable candelabrum
two metal or plastic candlecup holders, from florists
florists' extra-tacky fixing clay
pre-soaked moisture-holding florists' foam
florists' self–adhesive tape
a selection of evergreens and seasonal flowers such as
cypress, ivy, spray carnations, chrysanthemums,
carnations and alstroemeria
a 25 cm/10 inch candle, or size according to scale of design

Step 1 Press a thin strip of clay around the base of each holder. Press one 'cup' into each of the two outer candle cavities.

Step 2 Place a piece of pre-soaked foam into each holder. Secure it with two pieces of tape criss-crossed over the foam and on to the holder.

Step 3 Arrange the foliage and long, slender stems of buds and flowers so that they slant outwards and downwards at each side. Cut short sprays of evergreen leaves and press them into the foam so that the leaves cover and conceal it.

Step 4 Arrange larger, round and fully-opened flowers in the centre of the design to make a gentle, domed curve. Keep the foam topped up with water so that it is permanently moist.

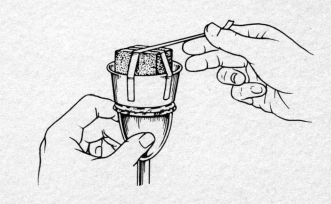

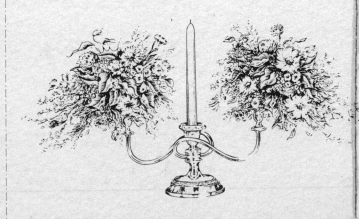

TRADITIONAL PASTIMES AND ENTERTAINMENTS

Beeton's Christmas Annuals included lots of ideas for family entertainment, from grand schemes for dramatic performances or charades acted out by several players to 'Nonsense Pages' with humorous passages, puzzles, limericks, cartoons and tricks. This final chapter provides an insight into the humour of Mrs Beeton's day.

Imagine the scene in the parlour, with the family gathered around the Christmas fire, adults and children alike contributing to the festive cheer. Reading was a favourite everyday activity and it was common practice for one member of the family to read aloud to the others. The annuals included suitable seasonal short stories, poems and the occasional light-hearted feature. The following is an extract from a humorous article entitled 'The Old, Old Tales.' These were introduced as having been 'translated from the original Chinese mss. looted by the writers at the ransacking of his celestial majesty's palace at Pekin. By Augustus Mayhew and The Odd Boy.'

The True Narrative of the Nuptials of Nisi Nisi and her wonderful Lover, the Frog Prince

The complete story is the familiar tale of the princess and the frog prince. The princess accidentally throws her ball into a lake but as she weeps a frog offers to retrieve it for her.

Beneath the shadow of the variegated peaks of yonder mountain, Nisi Nisi passed her silver childhood and her golden youth. She was beautiful as the rising of the sun, graceful as the tea-plant of Bohea. Sweetly, tunefully, and with unbroken voice, had she sung away the happy days of tender maidenship. Never as a lovely babe had she in the hours of nocturnal repose disturbed her revered parents; never had she caused them the bitter pang to which the parental heart only is susceptible, when infancy is wilful and violent. To her instructress, Snapi-Snarlee, she had ever been dutiful and obedient. She had ever done everything she was told to do; and never had she worn the cap of the simple one, nor stood in the corner penitential, nor been banished to repose at an early hour, nor shut up in the clothes-closet, to which roaring royal highnesses - her sisters - were oft condemned, and from when - through the keyhole - came the fervent promises of amendment, which sometimes, but not often, touched the heart of Snapi-Snarlee.

Stories which emphasised the virtues of good behaviour were considered suitable reading for young ladies and many Victorian stories devoted lengthy paragraphs to praising the heroine or expressing the gentlemanly nature of the hero. Following the above introduction, we eventually discover that the princess is in the garden playing, then there is another long account of her fine character before the story proper begins.

As Nisi Nisi played with her golden ball, it came to pass that it fell into the lake. The ripple of

the water, in expanding circle, marked the spot where it fell, and Nisi Nisi was in sore distress. Her eyes rained tears. But she recalled the saying of the sage, Liki-no-Liki, "Why should we mourn for the milk that is spilt?" Therefore, she wiped her eyes - likewise her nose - on the sleeve of her outer garment, and lo ! while she so did, she beheld a frog sitting on the edge of the lake, and which said unto her, "Why are thine eyes wet with tears?" "Because," she answered, "I have lost my ball." "What will you give me if I find it?" "O dear frog, I will give you my best thanks; my doll which is jointed - it has only lost its head and one arm; my tea-things - there's nothing missing but the milkpot and the cups and saucers; I will give you a taste of my fixed sweets."

The frog answered, "Not so, Nisi Nisi - dolls I cannot handle, tea-things are to me of no avail, and fixed sweets disagree with me. But give me yourself, pretty princess; let me be your playfellow; let me eat from your plate, drink from your cup, sit by your side, sleep in your bed - then will I bring back to you your golden ball."

The princess quickly agrees to the frog's request, then rushes off when her governess approaches, happy to have her ball again. Later at the dinner table, the princess is horrified when the frog approaches and asks her to keep her promise.

Nisi Nisi, is it to be?
Nisi Nisi, open to me!
You promised me by the garden wall
You would be my own if I found your ball;
Where are my chop-sticks?
Shuffle your mop-sticks:
To shut me out aint fair at all.

The princess is not allowed to escape her promise (another opportunity for a lecture on always keeping your word), so she dutifully allows the frog to share her food, her toys and her bed ... and, of course, the transformation to fine prince takes place.

Suddenly Nisi Nisi felt the cold frog grow warm, and swell; she did not know what to make of it, but said -

"Are you unwell, dear frog?"

He answered with a ringing laugh, and leapt from the bed - a frog no longer, but a handsome prince. Nisi Nisi screamed with delight; Snapi-Snarlee bounced in, with her hair in curl-papers, and bounced out again in a [The translator is unable to render this word in English, consequently gives the original - jiffee]. But the prince followed her and explained. A wicked Jaini had turned him into a frog, and as a frog he was condemned to remain until a beautiful and innocent young lady consented to take him for her own. This had been done by Nisi Nisi, and therefore was he restored to his proper form.

The prince and princess are married and there is a splendid description of the prince's fine clothes. The original story was brought to a close by an extract from one of the songs sung at the wedding feast.

Nisi Nisi and the young Prince were married. On the occasion of his wedding, the young Prince wore a dress composed of silks and crapes of great price; his feet were covered with high-heeled boots of the most beautiful Nankin satin; his legs were encased in gaiters, richly embroidered, and reaching to the knee. He had also an acorn-shaped cap of the latest taste; a pipe, richly ornamented; a toothpick, suspended to a button; and a Nankin fan, exhaling the perfume of the tcholane.

𝓕AMILY GAMES

Birds, Beast and Fishes

Form three teams: birds, beasts and fishes, and nominate a game leader. The leader is called Dr Livingstone and he or she makes up a story of travel all over the world, including encounters with animals birds and fishes. As Dr Livingstone mentions the birds, beasts and fishes, the appropriate team members have to respond ...

"All the Birds must flap their wings.
All the Beasts must go on all-fours.
All the Fishes must open their mouths,
and wag their tails.
And everyone must call out something
appropriate to his character."

The suggested appropriate cries included 'Ain't I fine?' for a bird of paradise; 'Pretty Poll' for a parrot; 'Hee-haw' for a donkey; 'Is dinner ready?' for a shark; and 'Gobble, gobble' for a turkey. Those who forget to respond to Dr Livingstone's prompts have to pay a forfeit.

Charades

Form two teams. Write words on pieces of paper, fold these and put them in a hat. Each team acts the word they pick out of hat. Each syllable in each word is acted separately in a short scene, then there is a final scene to bring the whole word together. Suitable words include crisis (cry, sis); determine (debt, ermine); fiddlesticks (fiddle, sticks); garden (guard, hen) and many more. Teams may dress up and really enter into the spirit of the acting. The more usual version of charades played today is for individuals to mime a word or phrase a syllable at a time, without speaking, indicating the first and consecutive syllables or words by holding up the appropriate number of fingers. If the teams take too long to guess, then set a time limit for the miming, with no points scored if the charade is not guessed within the permitted time.

Three Steps and A Kick

Place a mark on the floor, such as a piece of tape firmly pinned down, and fasten another marker at right angles from the middle of it to make a T shape. The cross piece should be about 30 cm/12 inches long and the stem of the T roughly 1 metre/1 yard long.

The player stands with the heel of the right foot on the cross piece and the foot on the stem. The player takes three steps along the stem, placing the heel to toe each time. Stand two wine corks on top of each other in front of the toe when the third step is taken. The player moves back behind the cross piece of the T and from this position he or she has to kick off the top wine cork, leaving the lower one in place without losing balance and without any support. After kicking off the cork, the player must stand still on the one foot on the ground for a count to ten - only then is the task considered complete. This may be performed by individuals or by teams.

Alliteration's Artful Art

Tongue-twisting phrases and passages were all part of the amusements in Beeton's Christmas Annual. Reading or repeating the phrases can be hilarious, especially when the company is split into two teams and each correct recital wins a point, every failed attempt means a forfeit. Write out a batch of suitable phrases to be picked out of a hat or allow teams to compose pieces for their opponents. For example:

Experienced economists enter each exact expenditure every evening.

Foolish flatterers find few firm friends, for faithfulness fearlessly follows fact.

Monied Maud's marriage made many maidens merry, more men mad.

Rascally rummaging rats run riot round ruined royal residences.

Quaint quiet Quakers quickly quell quibbling quacks' quarrelsome questions.

Unpunctuality unhappily undermines unnumbered useful undertakings.

Mother, age not asked.

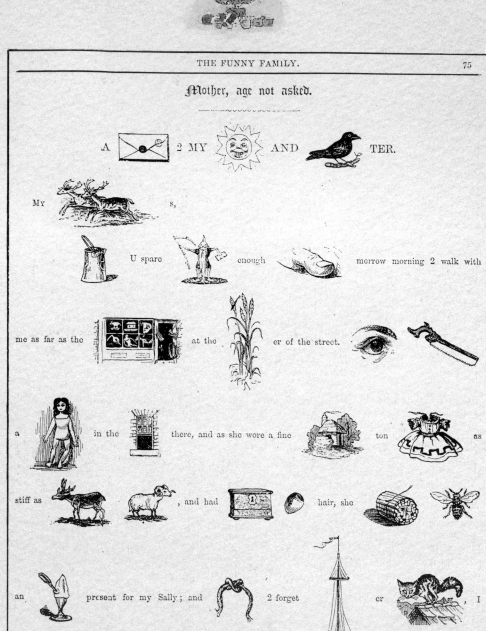

A ▢ 2 MY ☀ AND 🐦 TER.

My 🦌 s,

🪵 U spare 🧚 enough ✋ morrow morning 2 walk with

me as far as the 🖼 at the 🌽 er of the street. 👁 🪚

a 🪆 in the 🪟 there, and as she wore a fine 🛖 ton 👗 as

stiff as 🦌 🐏 , and had 🧰 🌰 hair, she 🪵 🐝

an present for my Sally ; and 〰 2 forget 🎪 , I

 also a and a that will him

👁 tally.

 THE FUNNY FAMILY.

 although I B lieve U will   with these presents, I could

write U quite a a of others I have store.

I d like to take U to the Play during U R days, as

 am   enough I will leave that 2 your 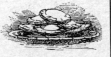 If you

do go, and C anything P Q liar or X N tric pl E E bring me a d account home.

I trust U will   eat 2 much nor too many

on Christmas day, it would not be comfor for U 2 take the day after.

With y good wishes,

I remain,

U R affectionate Mamma,

M E ly BOBBINSON.

P.S. BY UNCLE.—Do not leave the a w next U leave

the room.

Mrs Beeton's Traditional Christmas

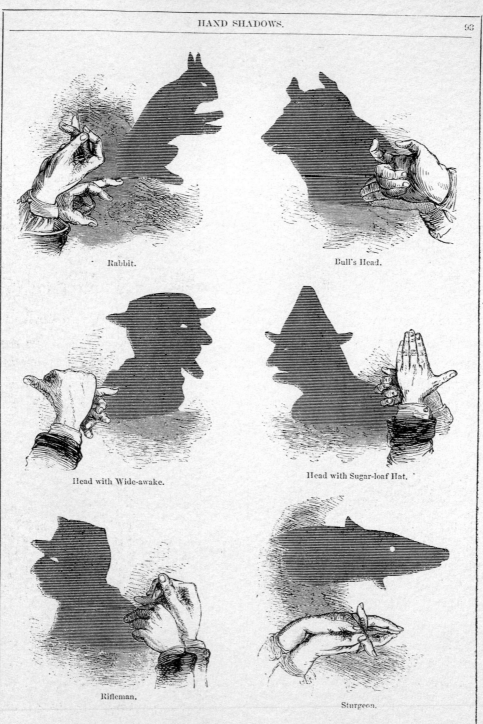

Rabbit.

Bull's Head.

Head with Wide-awake.

Head with Sugar-loaf Hat.

Rifleman.

Sturgeon.

NONSENSE PAGES

MUCH TOO GOOD TO BE LAUGHED AT

There was an incompetent mason,
Who instead of a cap wore a bason,
But some bricks falling down
On the top of his crown,
A catastrophe tended to hasten.

There once was an Absent Old Gent,
Who out for a day's shooting went;
But the Birds came and sat
On his Shoulders and Hat,
For he really forgot what he meant.

A Clown who has two little boys,
The whole of his leisure employs
In showing them how
To Mop and Mow,
Which increases their juvenile joys.

An Old maid with a chimney-pot hat,
Who had grown rather florid and fat,
Said, "My dear, at your age
You should not wear that cage."
But her friend merely said, "You old cat."

$\mathscr{S}$OLUTION TO PICTURE LETTER

The Picture Letter

A LETTER TO my SUN (son) and DAW (daugh)ter.

My DEER (Dear)s,

CAN U (you) spare TIME enough TOE (to)morrow morning TWO (to) walk with me as far as the TOYSHOP at the CORNer of the street? EYE (I) SAW a DOLL in the WINDOW there, and as she wore a fine COT ton FROCK as stiff as BUCK RAM, and had CHEST NUT hair, she WOOD (would) BEE (be) an (ICE) (a nice) present for my Sally; and KNOT (not) TWO (to) forget MAST er TOM, I SAW also a SWORD and a GUN that will SOOT (suit) him CAPEYE (capi)tally. BUTT (but) although I B (be) lieve U (you) will BEE (be) D LIGHTED (delighted) with these presents, I could write you quite a CAT a LOG (logue) of others

I have INN (in) store. ISHOEd (should) like to take U (you) to the play during U R (your) HOLLY (holi) days, BUTT (but) as EYE (I) am KNOT (not) well enough I will leave that TWO (to) your UNCLE. If you do go, and C (see) anything P Q liar (peculiar) or X N tric (eccentric), pl E E (please) bring me a SHREW d account home.

I trust U (you) will NOT (not) eat too much PLUM PUDDING nor too many MINCE PIES on Christmas-day; it would not be comfor TABLE for U (you) TWO (to) take PHYSIC the day after.

With HEART y good wishes,
I remain,
U R (your) affectionate Mamma,
M E ly (Emily) Bobbinson

P.S. by Uncle. - Do not leave the DOOR a JAR wHEN next U (you) leave the room.

INDEX